Beyond
Work–Family
Balance

Beyond
Work-Family
Balance

Advancing Gender Equity
and Workplace Performance

Rhona Rapoport
Lotte Bailyn
Joyce K. Fletcher
Bettye H. Pruitt

JOSSEY-BASS
A Wiley Company
www.josseybass.com

Published by

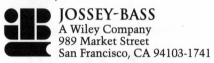 **JOSSEY-BASS**
A Wiley Company
989 Market Street
San Francisco, CA 94103-1741

www.josseybass.com

Copyright © 2002 by John Wiley & Sons, Inc.

Jossey-Bass is a registered trademark of John Wiley & Sons, Inc.

Jossey-Bass books and products are available through most bookstores. To contact Jossey-Bass directly, call (888) 378-2537, fax to (800) 605-2665, or visit our website at www.josseybass.com.

Substantial discounts on bulk quantities of Jossey-Bass books are available to corporations, professional associations, and other organizations. For details and discount information, contact the special sales department at Jossey-Bass.

We at Jossey-Bass strive to use the most environmentally sensitive paper stocks available to us. Our publications are printed on acid-free recycled stock whenever possible, and our paper always meets or exceeds minimum GPO and EPA requirements.

Library of Congress Cataloging-in-Publication Data

Beyond work-family balance : advancing gender equity and workplace performance /
    Rhona Rapoport ... [et al.].
        p. cm. — (Jossey-Bass business & management series)
        Includes bibliographical references and index.
        ISBN 0-7879-5730-5
        1. Sex discrimination in employment—United States. 2. Sex discrimination
    against women—United States. 3. Work and family—United States. I. Rapoport,
    Rhona. II. Series.
        HD6060.5.U5 B49 2002
        331.4'133'0973—dc21   2001005785

FIRST EDITION
HB Printing   10 9 8 7 6 5 4 3 2 1

The Jossey-Bass
Business & Management Series

Contents

To the four Bs

Preface

In 1990, June Zeitlin, a program officer of the Ford Foundation, launched a project that would take a different approach to the issue she had been calling work-family balance. Together with Rhona Rapoport, a longtime consultant to the Foundation on gender and work-family issues, she conceived a new initiative: a research partnership with for-profit corporations. For much of that year, Zeitlin and Rapoport made the rounds of corporate executive offices trying to identify a few large U.S. companies willing to participate. The organizations they approached were on the leading, progressive edge of work-family policy and offered an array of "family-friendly" benefits, such as parental leave, child and elder care resource and referral programs, and flexible schedules. But Zeitlin and Rapoport wanted to delve deeper—to look at organizational structures and the culture of work practices—in order to shed light on the sources of the widespread conflict between work and personal life, which, despite well-intended policies, stubbornly persisted.

The Ford Foundation itself had contributed substantially to the development of those progressive and innovative policies, as part of a long-term initiative to support the advance of women's rights on a broad front, including expanding their opportunities for employment. Focused at first on securing legal rights—for example, through equal-opportunity legislation—this initiative had moved on to address issues, such as the need for benefits and flexibility, raised by women's entrance into the workplace. Zeitlin's 1989 program paper, *Work and Family Responsibilities: Achieving a Balance,* provided an overview of this effort and the plans to continue it.

Yet by the end of the 1980s, it was evident that family-friendly policies alone were not sufficient. Few people were using them, and since nothing else had changed, those who were—mainly women—risked career repercussions. It seemed there was a need to make more systemic changes in work cultures and structures.

Tackling this complex problem clearly required the active participation of the companies under study. Zeitlin and Rapoport were proposing an "action research" approach, designed to generate new knowledge by changing a system and then studying the results. Outside researchers and company members would jointly identify the barriers in organizational structures and culture that were keeping people from using existing work-family policies. Together the researchers and their company partners would design experimental changes in work practices aimed at eliminating those barriers, and the researchers would track and assess the experiments and their effects. But the uncertainties in this approach made the project a tough sell to corporate executives. The researchers could not say at the start just what the work practice changes might be or what effect they might have on the organization's performance. As Zeitlin later wrote, "We were seeking to support companies that wanted to examine and were willing to try to change the work culture and organization of work. Still, no one was confident this could be done without negative consequences to the bottom line."[1]

Xerox Corporation was one of three companies that signed up to take a chance on this initiative. In 1991, a team of academic researchers co-led by Lotte Bailyn launched an action research project jointly with Xerox, which aimed to use work-family issues as a catalyst for organizational change at the level of work practices. Joyce Fletcher was a member of the team. Rhona Rapoport provided support and external perspective while serving as coordinator of the overall Ford Foundation–funded initiative. The Xerox project and its results—*in particular, the surprising and hopeful finding that it is possible to restructure work in ways that actually enhance organizational effectiveness while making the workplace more equitable and improving the quality of working people's lives*—provided the inspiration for this book, as well as much of the case material and methodological understanding it presents.[2]

This initial project and the others that followed made a significant departure from the established work-family field. In the first place, they reframed the issues in terms of gender, directing attention to the role played by strongly held, usually tacit, assumptions about how work should be done, assumptions that are linked to the traditional separation of work and family spheres and to stereotyped views of the roles of men and women in each. An example is the assumption that all employees fit the mold of the traditional middle-class married man: the family's sole breadwinner, for whom work is the highest priority and who is willing and able to devote whatever time and make whatever sacrifices might be called for to "get the job done." Such gendered assumptions—though they no longer fit, if they ever did, a large proportion of the workforce, male or female—are deeply embedded in work cultures, structures, and practices. They are largely responsible for persistent gender inequities in the workplace, and they are barriers to the success of work-family policies.

The Xerox project and others like it have also shown that these assumptions often support work practices that are inefficient and ineffective in the current work environment. Hence the unexpected linkage between improved performance on the one hand and greater gender equity, with reduced work–personal life conflict for everyone, on the other. In the Xerox project report, *Relinking Life and Work: Toward a Better Future* (1996), we identified in this linkage a "dual agenda" for organizational change. Since then, we have seen mounting evidence that the Dual Agenda is a valuable tool for improving organizational effectiveness while addressing the problems that work-family policies and benefits alone have proved unable to solve.

Our purpose in this book is to present the conceptual framework and the organizational change method behind the Dual Agenda and the results it has produced. We call this approach Collaborative Interactive Action Research (CIAR). In presenting CIAR, we are conscious of its emergent nature and of the many questions still to be answered about it, but we are confident that we are on the right track.

Most important, we have found that this method—by going to the level of the underlying assumptions about gender, work, and success that impede *both* equity *and* effectiveness in the workplace—can unlock tremendous creativity and energy for change. And although our focus has been on gender, there have been occasions when a Dual Agenda project has opened up space to examine other aspects of diversity as well. As we and others continue to develop this method, we hope to be able to expand that space so that the full range of equity issues can be raised and addressed. Yet we cannot wait to share it more broadly when at present both the need and the opportunity for change are great.

This book does not offer a simple prescription for how to achieve Dual Agenda results, because there is none. Each organization, and only the organization itself, has the requisite knowledge: the intimate understanding of the way its work gets done as well as access to the underlying assumptions dictating that the work must be done a particular way. The solutions one work group crafts for itself can suggest and inspire change in others but are not automatically transferable. What the book does offer, drawing on case material from projects in more than a dozen different workplace settings, are ways to think about this process so that organizations and the people in them who are so inclined may embark on a similar journey. We also share our understanding of some of the principles involved as well as the particular challenges we have encountered participating in Dual Agenda work.

All of this we present within a conceptual framework that addresses the question of why gender inequities and work–personal life conflict have been such intractable problems for our turn-of-the-century work organizations. Thus while we have no prescription, we do offer an analysis pointing to themes and issues that are common across many different organizational types and cultures. To the extent that this analysis rings true to our readers, we hope they will be motivated and armed to begin examining and questioning some of the unstated assumptions that govern how work is done in their own organizations, large and small, for profit and nonprofit.

We believe that many people may find this book of some interest: those concerned with gender equity; those wrestling on some level with issues of work-family or work-life "balance," which we call work–personal life integration; and those interested in organizational change. The analytical concepts and research findings we present are relevant to various disciplines—sociology, anthropology, management—and to all kinds of work organizations. The Dual Agenda message offers good news to forward-thinking CEOs, human resource personnel, and line managers that there need not be a trade-off between addressing employees' work–personal life conflicts and improving organizational performance. Though our research has focused primarily on the United States, it is relevant to other industrialized and industrializing countries as well.

Our hope is that any reader who has experienced gender inequity or work–personal life conflict will find the book a source of insight and ideas, which they may be able to use both in their own lives and in pressing for change in their workplaces. The results achieved so far offer encouragement, and the central chapters of this book provide a way to get started. The Appendix shows how the ideas and the method emerged and how they connect to similar work being pursued by others. As more people work with these ideas, they will continue to deepen the understanding of the method and its underlying principles and by doing so will push the boundaries of what is possible.

We are profoundly grateful to the many people who have worked with us and influenced our thinking on the issues discussed in this book. At one point, in the spirit of collaboration we consider so important to this effort, we tried to bring many of these people together in a joint effort to write this book. But it was not to be. We had a lively and valuable two-day retreat where we were joined by Deborah Kolb, Maureen Harvey, Roy Jacques, Jan Jaffe, Deborah Merrill-Sands, and Ann Rippin. Gill Coleman, though unable to join us at that time, contributed from a distance. Debra Meyerson and Robin Ely, who were not at the retreat, participated in an early planning meeting. These sessions produced insightful conversations and some chapter plans. But we could go no further. It seems we still have much to learn about what fosters and what impedes true collaborative effort.

Our gratitude to all these participants remains. We mention them here, refer to their published work throughout the book, and provide a bibliography of Dual Agenda–related writing. And in the Appendix, "The Book in Context," we acknowledge their contributions further, as part of an effort to illuminate the strands of theoretical and practical development that have come together to create a field of Dual Agenda work. Having just four authors has enabled us to achieve a level of synthesis and a clarity of voice that would likely not have been possible with a much larger group, but we are sensible of the loss of richness and multiple perspectives it also entails. We are also aware that publication brings up complicated issues of attribution, and we want to apologize immediately for any omissions.

The original Xerox action research team consisted of Lotte Bailyn, Susan Eaton, Joyce Fletcher, Maureen Harvey, Robin Johnson, Deborah Kolb, Leslie Perlow, and Rhona Rapoport, all of whom together created the insights from that project. At various points in some of this work we were also joined by Amy Andrews, Vicky Parker, and Mary Young, whom we thank for their efforts. Early on, we had the benefit of an advisory committee to the project, including Arlie Hochschild and Edgar H. Schein. Following the conclusion of the Xerox project, Deborah Kolb and Maureen Harvey continued to work with us for some time in a consulting group specializing in Dual Agenda work. And now we have been joined by Bettye H. Pruitt, who has enhanced our understanding of the method by helping us write about it.

Deborah Kolb brought a negotiation framework to the Xerox project and a keen conceptual eye. Since then, through her founding of the Center for Gender in Organizations at the Simmons Graduate School of Management, she and Deborah Merrill-Sands, her codirector, have brought together a group of people who have significantly contributed to our understanding of gender in organizations. Deborah Merrill-Sands has also led a number of Dual Agenda projects in which we have participated and gained much experience.

Maureen Harvey, a skilled interventionist, has participated in many of the projects described in this book and has helped us see things we were not always attuned to. Gill Coleman, Jan Jaffe, Roy Jacques, and Ann Rippin have brought thoughtful insights based on their own experiences. Gill Coleman also made a significant contribution to our understanding of the methodological context of CIAR, as did Mary Young. Robin Ely and Debra Meyerson have had important insights on these issues, and their approach intersects with ours in many ways. Debra Meyerson also played a leading role in one Dual Agenda project.

None of this work, it must be said, would have been possible without the full support, in so many different ways, of June Zeitlin and the Ford Foundation. We are grateful for June's imaginative vision and the willingness of the Ford Foundation to support such a risky enterprise as the Xerox project and subsequently to provide financial support for writing this book. The experiences of the two other teams originally funded by the foundation have also helped us understand the issues involved: Barbara Miller from Artemis and her team, especially Roy Jacques and Erica Pelavin; and Ellen Galinsky, Jim Levine, and Dana Friedman from the Families and Work Institute. And our gratitude goes to the people in the organizations we have worked with—our action partners—for putting up with us and learning with us.

Kathe Sweeney of Jossey-Bass has been a spirited champion of the ideas in this book, a sharp critic of our writing, and a helpful adviser. Her support throughout is much appreciated. And we are most grateful for the responsiveness of Jeff Wyneken during the production process. We also thank three anonymous reviewers whose detailed reports helped significantly in the final revisions.

We also want to thank each other for a valiant effort at collaboration. Each of us has played a different role in the production of this book: some have written more than others; some have edited or provided examples or kept the thinking clear and logical. In her own way, each has contributed equally to the final product.

Finally, we thank Bernard Bailyn, William C. Fletcher, and R. Bruce Pruitt, husbands who have lived the issues of gender equity and work–personal life integration with us, both personally and intellectually. Robert N. Rapoport, who died in 1996, deserves special acknowledgment. As the historical overview in the Appendix indicates, he was a full partner with Rhona in a long career of research and writing about work and family. He participated in originating the idea of writing this book, and his insights have informed both its spirit and its content. His continuing involvement was greatly missed.

October 2001   RHONA RAPOPORT
                                   LOTTE BAILYN
                                   JOYCE K. FLETCHER
                                   BETTYE H. PRUITT

The Authors

Rhona Rapoport is director of the Institute of Family and Environmental Research, a nonprofit educational trust located in London. In 1994–95 she was a scholar in residence at the Ford Foundation, and in recent years she has been a Distinguished Fellow and adviser at the Center for Gender in Organizations at the Simmons Graduate School of Management in Boston. Born in Cape Town, South Africa, she earned her bachelor of social science degree at the University of Cape Town and her doctorate in sociology at the London School of Economics. She subsequently completed training as a psychoanalyst at the London Institute of Psychoanalysis. Her publications—many written in collaboration with her late husband, Robert—include *Dual Career Families* (Penguin Books, 1971); *Leisure and the Family Life Cycle* (Routledge & Kegan Paul, 1975); *Fathers, Mothers and Society* (Basic Books, 1977); and with Peter Moss, *Men and Women as Equals at Work* (Thomas Coram, 1990). For twenty years, she has been a consultant to the Ford Foundation working on affirmative action programs in the United States and in developing countries and on work and family issues. A major concern in her work is the issue of equity between men and women. To this end, she has collaborated with action research projects in the United States and England, as well as on the development of

a training program on organizational change and work-family issues for advancing diverse groups in the new South Africa. She
is currently engaged in a review of the movement on work–
personal life integration, *Looking Backward to Go Forward*.

Lotte Bailyn is the T Wilson (1953) Professor of Management
at MIT's Sloan School of Management, where she has taught
for thirty years. She holds a bachelor of arts degree from Swarth-
more College in mathematics and a doctorate from Harvard in
social psychology and is a Fellow of the American Psychologi-
cal Association. Her primary interest is in the conditions of work
and how they affect the careers and lives of technical and managerial professionals. Her research deals with the relation of
organizational practice to employees' personal lives and has
emphasized such workplace innovations as telecommuting,
flexible scheduling, work-family benefits, and work redesign.
She is the author of numerous articles and a number of books,
including *Living with Technology: Issues at Mid-Career* (MIT
Press, 1980), and coauthor of *Working with Careers* (Columbia
University Press, 1984). Her book *Breaking the Mold: Women,
Men, and Time in the New Corporate World* (Free Press, 1993)
sets out the hypothesis that by challenging the assumptions in
which current work practices are embedded, it is possible not
only to meet the goals of both business productivity and employees' family and community concerns but also to do so in
ways that are equitable for men and women. The book spells
out the contours of how this might be done, and the work she
and others have been engaged in during the past decade, much
of it detailed in this book, has supported this basic proposition.

Joyce K. Fletcher is professor of management at the Center for
Gender in Organizations, Simmons Graduate School of Man-

agement, Boston, and a senior research scholar at the Jean Baker Miller Training Institute at the Wellesley College Centers for Women. Before coming to CGO, she spent fifteen years as an associate professor of cooperative education for the College of Business Administration at Northeastern University. She received her doctoral degree in organizational behavior from Boston University's School of Management, and her dissertation, "Toward a Theory of Relational Practice: A Feminist Reconstruction of 'Real' Work," explored the social construction of gender in the workplace. Fletcher teaches courses in organizational behavior, specializing in the effective leadership of individuals and groups. In her research, she uses relational theory to study a wide range of workplace issues, including motivation, power, influence, equity, and gender. She has consulted in both the corporate and not-for-profit worlds and has published widely in education and management journals, including the *Harvard Business Review*. She is a frequent speaker at national and international conferences on the topic of women, power, and leadership. Her recent book, *Disappearing Acts: Gender, Power, and Relational Practice at Work* (MIT Press, 1999) — which was designated a finalist for the 2001 George R. Terry Book Award for outstanding contribution to the advancement of management knowledge, presented annually by the Academy of Management — addresses the subtle dynamics that often "disappear" women's leadership behavior at work and suggests practical strategies to enhance personal and organizational success.

Bettye H. Pruitt is the president of Pruitt & Company, Inc., a research and consulting firm devoted to realizing the practical value of history in organizations, and a trustee of the Society for Organizational Learning. She holds a doctorate in history from Boston University and has worked in the field of organizational history since 1983, writing both published and proprietary works of critical history for a diverse group of clients. A longtime focus of her work has been the development of an approach to creating project histories that support team learning and accomplishment in real time as well as reflection and communication after the project's conclusion. Much of her current efforts are devoted to supporting learning and action in the civic realm. Some of these histories have been published on the Internet, at www.undp.org/rblac/scenarios/report and www.bostonstrategy.com. Before creating Pruitt & Company, in 1998, she was managing partner of The Winthrop Group, Inc., a business consulting firm specializing in historical analysis of institutional issues and development. Recent Winthrop Group–related publications include *Timken: From Missouri to Mars—A Century of Leadership in Manufacturing* (Harvard Business School Press, 1998) and "Our Evolving Understanding of the Value of History for Hire," *Essays in Business and Economic History* (1997).

Beyond
Work – Family
Balance

CHAPTER 1

Introduction: The Equity Imperative

This book is about advancing gender equity in work organizations and enabling men and women to resolve the often painful conflict, endemic in industrialized societies, between work and personal life. And it is about doing so in a way that enhances workplace performance. Our goal is to move the discourse on these issues beyond the simple work-family (or work-life) dichotomy by reaching deeper and focusing attention on the underlying assumptions about men's and women's roles in family, community, and paid work, assumptions that shape our workplaces as they shape all our social institutions. Family-friendly policies in progressive companies have brought us part of the way toward making organizations hospitable to people who want both to work and to "have a life." But even the most advanced workplaces have not probed the assumptions that give rise to the basic problems of gender equity. Only by establishing the link between current work practices and gendered assumptions about the role and organization of work will it be possible to identify major leverage points for significant, constructive change. This is true, we believe, in all industrialized and industrializing societies, but none more so than in the United States, where most of our research has taken place.

The Equity Imperative

By our definition, advancing gender equity in the workplace involves, first, challenging organizational norms that assume the primacy of paid work in working people's lives and that limit the career choices and opportunities of those who seek fulfillment through commitments in *both* work and personal life. Second, it means valuing diverse ways of working, recognizing and rewarding the full range of skills and contributions that people bring to an organization's success. Our definition, we realize, is culture-bound. It has emerged in response to conditions in Western, capitalist, corporate work organizations that have, historically, been directed and shaped by white, married, middle-class men—people for whom paid work *has* been primary and whose characteristic strengths and skills have been enshrined in corporate cultures and reward systems. But in twenty-first-century workplaces, these established norms are problematic, not just for women, but for many men who do not fit the traditional mold. As a result, there is mounting pressure on work organizations to deal more effectively with gender equity and work–personal life issues.

External Pressures for Change

It has been clear for some time now that organizations in the United States have responded inadequately to the twin challenges of the late twentieth century: greater diversity of the work-force—in particular the large influx of women—and global-ization. Although diversity is greater at entry levels, we have come up short on the promise of equal opportunity. Positions of power are still primarily held by a largely homogeneous group of white men, despite antidiscrimination legislation and the establishment of "family-friendly" policies in many leading corporations. At the same time, women, men, and the society as a whole are suffering from the steady increase of working hours for most employees that has been an unfortunate by-product of the way organizations have adapted to globalization.

U.S. corporations justify demanding more and more from their workforce by pointing to the threat from Japanese and western European competitors, while companies in those countries cite the threat from the United States and each other. Few have had the courage to step off this destructive path or the vision to see that doing so might offer a competitive advantage.[1] The U.S. workforce now logs more time on the job each year than workers in any other industrialized nation, and stress from overwork is widespread. Here again, legislative and policy solutions—like the 1993 Medical and Family Leave Act and progressive company programs offering employees leaves and flexible work arrangements—though necessary, have proved insufficient.

The shortfall of these well-intended policy-level approaches has left many people feeling disillusioned and angry about persistent workplace inequities and overwork. Companies that have been leaders in adopting policies on leaves and flexible hours are coming under attack for the "gap" between these formal policies and "actual practices." Critics dismiss their efforts to be family-friendly as "just a public relations or recruiting tool."[2]

Political polling in the United States in the 2000 presidential election year indicated that equal pay, benefits, and flexibility in managing work and family are high-priority issues for women and that a majority of women believe government can and should play a role in helping them achieve those objectives.[3] Coincidentally, the August 2000 edition of *Good Housekeeping* magazine reported survey results showing 86 percent of women frequently feeling tired and stressed by the competing demands of work and personal life and revealing high levels of alcohol use, overeating, lack of time for regular medical checkups, lack of interest in sex, and suicidal feelings. A 2001 poll by the National Sleep Foundation corroborated those findings and expanded them to include men as well as women, finding that 38 percent of adults spend fifty hours or more per week at work and all adults "spend less time involved in leisure and social activities, having sex, and sleeping compared to five years ago."[4]

These data capture problematic trends that could translate into political will if politicians were to take up this issue as Mona Harrington, for example, suggests they should. In *Care and Equality*, Harrington notes the social costs of the failure to find an adequate "equality-respecting" system for care, particularly child care, to replace the one that existed when most women worked full time at home. A political agenda to deal with the problem, she suggests, should focus on changes in the workplace, "because it is hours of work and wage levels that have the most direct effect on the way families can organize their lives. . . . The reigning idea that the sole corporate responsibility is to create value for shareholders must be replaced by one that expands corporate obligation to include social health—and that means an obligation to support families and care."[5]

Governments in Europe are already more engaged in these issues. Sweden and Norway have long had legislated parental leave policies, which they continue to refine and expand. Legislation proposed in Great Britain and the Netherlands to guarantee a universal right to part-time work aims at a political remedy for work–personal life conflicts. France is experimenting with a thirty-five-hour workweek. These are potential models for legislative initiatives in the United States. Alternatively, civil rights lawyer Joan Williams maps out a plausible litigation strategy for using the provisions of existing U.S. antidiscrimination laws to force changes in workplace norms that penalize people who do not fit the traditional mold of the "ideal" worker—someone who is willing and able to put work above all other considerations.[6]

There is also external pressure from the changing business environment in which all work organizations must operate. On the one hand, there is the need to work more openly and more collaboratively with outsiders, such as customers, suppliers, merger partners, joint-venture partners, and sometimes even competitors. On the other hand, increased competition necessitates communication and collaboration inside the organization—across functions, between divisions, within teams. To develop these essential capabilities, organizations need employees with relational skills, skills that have traditionally been cultivated in the "feminine" sphere of caring relationships and neglected in the "masculine" sphere of paid work. This means, at the very least, that organizations must get better at recognizing and rewarding those skills. Beyond that, we believe they should look at ways in which workplace norms of overwork undermine the development of relational skills by making it difficult or impossible for employees to invest significant time in activities that help them do so, such as participation in family and community life.

Internal Pressures for Change

Quite apart from these external pressures is the imperative from within organizations to enable all of their employees to perform up to their potential. The persistence of the "glass ceiling" despite efforts to recruit, retain, and advance women in professional and managerial ranks represents significant costs to organizations—both the measurable cost of developing individuals who then choose to forgo or abandon ambitious career paths and the immeasurable cost of the loss of talent their choices entail. Moreover, despite the myth to the contrary, it is not only women who are feeling the conflict between work and personal life. A key finding of the Families and Work Institute's Fatherhood Project, for example, is that many men are suffering in silence, afraid to talk about the stress of being a parent in a two-career family.[7]

We have seen some high-profile rejections of the ideal worker norm, such as Fidelity Investments' Peter Lynch stepping off the fast track to devote more time to family and community. In a 2000 commencement address, William Rehnquist, chief justice of the United States Supreme Court, urged graduating law students to consider the drawbacks of high-flying legal careers, such as "the relentless demand for billable hours, which may leave less time than one would like for a personal life."[8] And Robert Reich, in *The Future of Success*, explains that family was the prime reason he left what he called the best job he ever had—U.S. secretary of labor in the Clinton administration.[9]

These examples suggest it may soon become much more acceptable for men, too, to opt out of unyielding, overly demanding jobs.

There are also significant costs to organizations associated with employees who stay in their jobs and meet all the demands of work in our globalized, downsized economy. In 1997, the World Bank held a symposium on stress, the business traveler, and corporate health in order "to make employers think more responsibly about the effect of ever-increasing travel . . . on employees and the people closest to them."[10] A clinical study sponsored for this symposium found higher rates of insurance claims among frequent travelers, particularly those who thought of themselves as tough and resilient. A study published in July 2000 by the Analysis Group and MIT's Sloan School of Management on the monetary impact of employee stress indicated that each employee suffering from stress-related depression cost his or her employer $3,000 a year.[11] A 2001 survey by the Families and Work Institute showed that nearly half of all U.S. workers felt overworked and that work-related stress was associated with increased mistakes on the job, as well as higher health care costs and the costs of training new people to replace those who leave because of burnout.[12]

Finally, we predict that an increasing source of competitive pressure will come from pioneering companies that, like SAS Institute, Inc., are responding in creative ways to these realities. Heralded by *Fast Company* magazine as "Sanity Inc.," SAS has demonstrated that work–personal life integration can be a corporate priority coexisting with high levels of performance, as well as employee loyalty.[13] Even more encouraging, recent research done by Marian Ruderman and Patricia Ohlott at the Center for Creative Leadership indicates that having multiple roles is significantly correlated with high performance. In their book *Standing at the Crossroads*, they describe the specific skills and capabilities people acquire from these multiple roles, especially their roles as caregivers in family and community.[14]

Global Considerations

With the end of the Cold War and the triumph of capitalism, the corporate model of operational effectiveness is without significant challengers. In the United States, it has moved across boundaries, for example, into health care and education. It has become even more prominent with the ascent to power of President George W. Bush, who holds a master's degree in business administration and has set out to govern in the mode of a corporate chief executive officer.[15]

The corporate model is also spreading internationally as part of globalization, and there is grave danger in the rapid, uncritical adoption of this model, which, from the perspective of working men and women, has serious defects as well as significant advantages. We do not wish to see the inequitable and un-family-friendly aspects of the corporate model spread across human society. Yet this is already occurring. For example, the 1999 World Development Report of the United Nations Development Programme describes how the crisis of care is spreading to developing countries, threatening traditional cultures and exacerbating problems of poverty.[16] As globalization continues apace, it is more important than ever to challenge the organizational norms that create these patterns. We believe that an effective way to do so is through the pursuit of gender equity.

Beyond Work-Family to Gender Equity

As our framing of the equity imperative suggests, our thinking about equity and our approach to achieving it are intimately bound up with work-family concerns. At the same time, those concerns are inextricably linked to underlying issues of gender and gender equity. A central message of this book is that the greatest opportunity for change at this point in time lies in going to those deeper issues of how people perceive men's and women's roles in both the work and domestic spheres. Those perceptions largely determine what is possible in each, in part because they are embedded in established structures, relationships, and ways of doing things and in part because they exert powerful influence over people's sense of identity and self-esteem. Finding a way to bring to the surface and to work constructively with those underlying patterns is thus one of the surest—though also one of the most challenging—routes to making some of the changes that have so far eluded work-family initiatives.

Defining Gender and Gender Equity

Gender used to be a grammatical term. There are old manuals on English usage that specifically say to use *gender* only to refer to nouns, not people. But as the research on women began to build up over the second half of the twentieth century, theorists began to differentiate *gender* from *sex:* both were applicable to human beings but signified different things. *Sex* was to refer to the biological difference between men and women, whereas *gender* referred to the socially constructed understanding of what it meant to be a man or a woman. Thus gender dealt with masculine and feminine stereotypes—for example, men are strong, active, aggressive, rational, and calculating; women are weak, passive, supportive, emotional, and impulsive.

Lately, gender theorists have come to see gender as an organizing principle of society. But in the public domain, *gender* has almost completely replaced *sex* in common usage and too often is seen as synonymous with *female*. Indeed, we have heard that in one country trying to accommodate its English-speaking visitors, one bathroom was labeled "men" and the other one "gender"! Just as white people often do not see themselves as having a race, so men often do not see themselves as having a gender.

We use the term quite differently. We use it to apply to both men and women and to refer to the socially constructed categories of masculinity and femininity. However, in discussing masculine and feminine norms, we do not mean to imply that all men and women conform to those stereotypes or act in stereotypical ways. Our meaning is simply that these norms dictate *expectations* of male and female characteristics and of how men and women will act in various situations and settings. In pointing out the need to challenge masculine gendered norms in the workplace, we do not envision their being supplanted by feminine ones. Rather, our aim is to promote the creation of new and more innovative work practices in both spheres of life that are based on the needs of the work and not on gender stereotypes and gender expectations, masculine or feminine.[17]

Gender equity, as we use the term, means a fair allocation of opportunities and constraints for men and women in all spheres. We emphasize fairness rather than equality partly to honor the reality that different life goals and priorities, as well as differing capabilities, shape individuals' wants and needs at work, as in life as a whole. In addition, we have seen how a focus on equality can promote sameness in ways that lead inadvertently to unfair outcomes. An example is women gaining equal access to jobs that require long hours at work without complementary changes in social norms around the sharing of household responsibilities—a phenomenon that has made home life into an onerous "second shift" for many working women. Another example is policies that supposedly give all employees the opportunity to negotiate parental leave and flexible schedules but, in the absence of changes in expectations for male behavior at work, have been largely off-limits to men.[18]

We also do not mean to say that gender is the only equity issue in the workplace or necessarily the most important. Nor do we mean to imply that workplaces are the only social institutions that need to change in order to achieve it. Yet we have found that looking at work practices and organizational cultures through a gender lens is a powerful lever for opening up the question of whether work as currently organized is as it has to be.

Connections to the Work-Family Field

Using a gender lens brings many issues to the fore, but none more frequently than work patterns that create painful conflicts between work and personal life for both men and women. As a result, our efforts are strongly aligned with—and have contributed to—the now well-established field of work and family.

An early statement on "work and family in contemporary society" came in the 1960s from Rhona and Robert Rapoport. They later coined the term *dual-career families* in their 1971 book by that name, which examined issues of gender equity and work–personal life conflict from the perspective of professional couples in Britain.[19] This was in an era when work and family were separate fields in sociology and psychology, and there was little conceptual linkage between them. The Rapoports were part of a small group of researchers — including some in the United States and some in Sweden — who were beginning to look at gender roles across this work-family divide.[20]

In 1977, Rosabeth Moss Kanter provided the first full-scale review of work-family interactions in her book *Work and Family in the United States*, contributing to "work and family" as an emerging field of study and concern. Her *Men and Women of the Corporation*, published the same year, was an early exploration of gender issues in the workplace, a topic taken up by a few feminist scholars in the 1980s. Subsequently, Arlie Hochschild's *The Second Shift: Working Parents and the Revolution at Home* (1989), Juliet Schor's *The Overworked American: The Unexpected Decline of Leisure* (1991), and Lotte Bailyn's *Breaking the Mold: Women, Men, and Time in the New Corporate World* (1993) moved the field forward conceptually by looking more deeply at the way cultural norms in families and workplaces contributed to work–personal life conflicts and gender inequity.[21] More recently, a number of significant additions to our understanding of the gender issues in family and work have come from Mona Harrington's *Care and Equality: Inventing a New Family Politics* (1999), Joyce K. Fletcher's *Disappearing Acts: Gender, Power, and Relational Practice at Work* (1999), and Joan Williams's *Unbending Gender: Why Family and Work Conflict and What to Do About It* (2000).[22]

In the realm of policy, work-family issues became an area of focus in the 1980s as people began to realize that the enactment of equal-opportunity legislation, in the 1970s, was not by itself sufficient to secure a place for women in the workforce. A number of institutions have played a central role in this field. The Ford Foundation was an early, major supporter of policy development and research. The Families and Work Institute, with substantial Ford Foundation funding, has been a leader in developing and evaluating family-friendly policies and has conducted essential research, including studies of the changing role of fathers and, more recently, of children's attitudes toward their parents' work. Catalyst and the Conference Board are other nonprofit organizations that early on started collecting data on these issues and are still important contributors to the field. A pioneering consulting firm, Work/Family Directions, still continues its work and has now been joined by many others.

More recently, the Alfred P. Sloan Foundation has provided additional impetus to work-family research. Its Working Families Area, led by Kathleen Christensen, has established Alfred P. Sloan Centers for Working Families at the University of California, Berkeley, for the examination of the culture of care, working parents, and childhood; at the University of Michigan for the ethnography of everyday life; at the University of Chicago for the study, by means of experience sampling, of parents, children, and work; at Cornell for the study of employment and family careers across the life course; at Emory for the study of rituals and myths in working families; and at the University of California, Los Angeles, for video ethnographies of the everyday life of working families. The Sloan Foundation also supports the Sloan Work and Family Research Network at Boston College (http://www.bc.edu/wfnetwork), which provides on-line resources and opportunities for researchers and others interested in work and family issues, as well as many individual research efforts in a number of different institutions.[23]

These are just a few examples of activities in a field that continues to expand steadily. Other universities, nonprofit organizations, consulting firms, government agencies, unions, and professional organizations, as well as numerous publications, both electronic and print, deal with work-family issues.[24] Collectively, all of this effort has created a supportive context for addressing issues of gender equity and work–personal life conflict, both within organizations and in society at large. And it is within that context that our ideas and approach have emerged.

The immediate impetus to the research reported here grew out of the Ford Foundation's Women's Program and its Women's Program Forum, established in 1986. In 1989, the Forum provided an opportunity to examine the current debates and possible responses to the growing needs of men and women for "balancing" their work and family responsibilities. This effort reaffirmed that women were not being treated equitably with men in the workplace. Not only were there issues of unequal pay and unequal access to career mobility, but there seemed to be continued gender stereotyping and — important for our purposes — disincentives to using work-family programs and policies in ways that could decrease inequities. Even in organizations that had well-developed work-family policies and benefits, men and women fared differently. Such organizations were also losing the women they wanted to keep and thus had begun to realize that the work-family programs they had developed were not achieving the intended results.[25]

These conclusions set the stage for a new Ford Foundation initiative in the early 1990s, a multiyear research collaboration with three large U.S. corporations: Corning, Inc.; Xerox Corporation; and Tandem Corporation. Its goal was to find an explanation for the disappointing results of work-family policies by taking a critical look at work structure and practices and at the culture surrounding them. The formative research behind the conceptual framework and organizational change method presented here took place within the Xerox project. Informed by the evolving understanding of gender issues in the work-family field, as we have just described, the research team members and their organizational partners jointly framed this project as an effort to use work-family issues as a catalyst for innovation in work practices. They aimed to test the hypothesis that such innovations could serve multiple ends—enhancing productivity as well as ensuring gender equity and easing the conflict between work and personal life.

The final report on this initiative, *Relinking Life and Work: Toward a Better Future*, published by the Ford Foundation in 1996, was the first public statement of the positive results emerging from this research. It laid the foundation for moving beyond the work-family frame and, in particular, beyond the concept of balance.[26]

Beyond Balance

Clearly, our focus on gender equity in the workplace is connected to the work-family field, and our concerns certainly embrace the issues traditionally included in it. Protecting families and legitimating the claims of family responsibilities are critical objectives we share. Yet we eschew the term *work-family balance*—as well as the related and currently more popular *work-life balance*—in order to emphasize some key principles.

As a matter of principle, our concept of equity suggests the need to honor the full diversity of personal-life arrangements in the workplace. We want to be explicit about pursuing changes in organizations that will address the concerns of single people and couples with no children, as well as those of working parents. Only by challenging underlying assumptions about the totally work-involved ideal worker in the broadest possible terms will it be possible to avoid the danger of simply shifting the burden of meeting unreasonable expectations from parents to non-parents. At the level of changing work practices, where we focus our attention, success comes when everyone is engaged in making changes aimed at providing some benefits to all. In contrast, we have observed that defining work–personal life dilemmas as family issues, and by implication as women's issues, has tended in the past to marginalize them—a phenomenon that has limited the effect of family-friendly policies and created inequities. Thinking and speaking in terms of work–personal life issues, instead of work and family, has helped us keep these distinctions clearly in view.

We also wanted to develop an alternative to the phrase *work-life balance*, which implies that work is not part of life and that everyone's time should be split equally between the two. On the contrary, paid work *is* a part of life—a necessary one for most adults and often a meaningful and rewarding one as well. Indeed, the essence of strategies widely adopted in U.S. companies in the 1980s and 1990s to increase their competitiveness has been to make work more meaningful for more people through employee empowerment and alignment with organizational goals. The implications of this shift for workers is captured in the contrast drawn by a shop-floor employee in a manufacturing plant that had implemented self-directed teams. "I hired into the machine shop and came in and did the same thing every day. I had no responsibilities. I just did the job and went home. Today I've changed dramatically, and the reason is that they laid a lot of responsibility on me. Now I see a problem and I try to do something about it. I've become a lot smarter because of that responsibility."

Yet changes such as this individual experienced have also tended to mean more stress and more time on the job. *Fast Company*, a popular new magazine of the late 1990s, exudes the complex reality of the so-called New Economy, of which the empowered worker is the foundation. In virtually every issue, there are versions of dueling mantras: "You are your work!" and "Get a life!" *Fast Company* makes no effort to resolve the tension between the two. But individuals—and organizations—must.

The fact is that not everyone wants to give equal weight to work and personal life, but this should not mean that choosing one requires sacrificing the other. Accepting that individual priorities differ, our goal is that men and women should be able to experience these two parts of their lives as not in conflict, or separate and in need of balance, but *integrated*. By this we mean that they should be able to function and find satisfaction in *both* work and personal life, independent of the amount of time they actually spend in each domain at different stages of their lives.

In Chapter Two, we describe more fully what we see when we look at work through a gender lens and further develop our vision of work–personal life integration. We believe that this vision is attainable because, as it turns out, the assumptions and norms that block gender equity in the workplace also undermine people's productivity. Thus one of the most surprising and heartening results of our research has been the discovery of the link between gender equity and organizational effectiveness.

Linking Gender Equity and Workplace Performance: The Dual Agenda

Our approach differs from other gender equity and work-family initiatives in that it focuses on the way work is done and links the goal of increasing gender equity and work–personal life integration to the goal of improved workplace performance in what we call the Dual Agenda. In part, our method resides within the body of organizational change work—including, for example, organizational learning—that connects humanistic values with the goal of helping people learn how to work more effectively.[27] Our approach differs from these in significant ways, however, because of our explicit focus on gender and the way gendered assumptions about ideal workers, ideal work, and ideal leaders may be powerfully—albeit invisibly—inhibiting such positive connections.[28]

The Dual Agenda

The concept of the Dual Agenda is based on the finding that working on gender equity issues by challenging entrenched organizational norms opens up consideration of the ways in which those norms undermine the work as well as the people who do it. Questioning the assumption that time spent at work is a good measure of commitment, for example, can get people thinking about how much time really *is* required to accomplish a particular job. They may then see how much time they may be wasting with inefficient practices developed in the context of seemingly unlimited available time—a context dependent on the norm of an ideal worker who is both willing and able to give priority to workplace demands above all others. Likewise, a frank examination of how formal and informal definitions of job requirements tacitly favor stereotypical masculine ways of working—say, in a mode of heroic individualism—can uncover ways in which jobs might be done better if a broader range of capabilities and approaches were considered.

In short, looking at work through a lens of gender equity or work–personal life integration can bring into focus obstacles to effectiveness that usually remain hidden because they are unquestioned—they are simply "the way it is." Far from undermining performance, taking up these issues can go a long way toward improving it. In Chapter Three, we examine this surprising and significant finding and its implications.

The idea of the Dual Agenda emerged in the Ford Foundation–funded Xerox project of the early 1990s. Since then, numerous other projects have confirmed its validity. The Gender Staffing Program of the Consultative Group on International Agricultural Research; the Center for Gender in Organizations at the Graduate Management School of Simmons College; the Public Policy Center of the Radcliffe Institute for Advanced Studies at Harvard University; LUME International, LLP, a consulting partnership that for a few years carried out Dual Agenda projects; and Artemis Management Consultants, a research partner with Tandem Corporation in the original Ford Foundation initiative, have all carried out such projects, in a number of cases with further support from the Ford Foundation. Their organizational partners have included for-profit corporations such as The Body Shop International, Fleet Financial Group, DTE Energy, and HP/Agilent, as well as nonprofits and nongovernmental development organizations such as CIMMYT and BRAC.[29]

These projects provide the case material presented in this book, and collectively they have also furthered the development of the method used to achieve Dual Agenda results—Collaborative Interactive Action Research (CIAR). We offer a brief introduction of this approach here and present it more fully in the three central chapters of the book. Although the results of Dual Agenda projects have been reported in many places, and some of the publications have described the method used, this book represents the first attempt to present it in detail and to share what we have learned so far.

Collaborative Interactive Action Research (CIAR)

The method we have evolved is a combination of interactive collaboration and action research. This method works because it lets us uncover and work with underlying assumptions and feelings about gender, work, and success that impede both equity and performance in the workplace. Although it is not easy to keep the equity and work effectiveness goals on the table at all times, it is essential for the kind of change we aim to produce. In that sense, our method and our Dual Agenda mission are inextricable.

Briefly, the CIAR approach starts out with an inquiry phase, in which the action researchers become acquainted with the organization's culture, work, and work practices and begin to understand individual employees' equity and work–personal life issues. Inquiry activities include individual interviews across levels and functions, small group discussions, and observation of work practices. Throughout these interactions, the researchers work collaboratively with people in the organization to identify themes, underlying assumptions, and potential leverage points for change. An analysis of Dual Agenda issues (those with implications for both equity and effectiveness) emerges iteratively as researchers share preliminary findings, test ideas, and develop them further with input from the organization.

The process culminates in a feedback session, the purpose of which is to highlight underlying assumptions, making the connection between work practices and equity issues as they are experienced in the organizational system. Taboo topics—concerns that individuals had not previously been able to raise publicly—become explicit during the feedback session and legitimately discussable. This formal presentation of the researchers' analysis to the group as a whole is also another point of collaborative interaction, and a critical one, as people in the organization discuss the researchers' findings and interpretation and together reach an understanding of what they mean. From feedback and collective interpretation, this session, ideally, moves directly into defining Dual Agenda change in work practices. For example, at one site, a product development team decided to restructure the rhythm of its daily activities to allow a period of uninterrupted concentration on core tasks. At another site, a financial unit decided to shift the allocation of tasks between professionals and support staff in order to give the professionals more time to work with customers and the support staff an opportunity for career development. In both cases, the work groups aimed explicitly to improve their performance while enabling both men and women to do their jobs with less stress and more control over their time and the conditions of their work.

Such seemingly simple adjustments in work practices can be surprisingly effective for both sides of the Dual Agenda. Yet implementing such changes typically uncovers new layers of underlying assumptions, which crop up to reassert established work patterns even though they might be suboptimal. An important part of CIAR thus involves continuing to work toward understanding those assumptions better, getting the experience of bringing them to explicit awareness and making concrete changes that challenge them, and working with the feelings they invoke.

Conclusion

This book is about increasing gender equity and work–personal life integration in work organizations through the use of Collaborative Interactive Action Research. Drawing on case material from projects in more than a dozen different organizational settings, we show that it is possible to restructure work in ways that enhance organizational effectiveness while making the workplace more equitable. That is the Dual Agenda.

The concepts and method we present here have emerged from a long stream of research in the work-family field and embrace work-family concerns. But we also look beyond those concerns to the underlying assumptions about work that create often painful work–personal life conflicts for parents and non-parents alike. Because of the way work organizations have evolved in Western industrialized societies (in the social context of rigid separation between the masculine sphere of paid work and the feminine domestic sphere), those underlying assumptions are gendered. It is for this reason that focusing on gender equity, as we do in CIAR, provides significant leverage on problems that family-friendly policies and benefits have inadequately addressed. In Chapter Two, we look more closely at key gendered assumptions, where they come from, and how they affect both equity and organizational effectiveness.

PART 1

Context and Concepts

CHAPTER 2

Pursuing Equity in Gendered Organizations

Gender inequities in the workplace do not exist in isolation but are part of the social fabric. They are rooted in the historic separation of spheres—the masculine sphere of paid work and the feminine sphere of domestic life—and are maintained through a variety of beliefs and cultural assumptions that underpin workplace practices. The reality today is much more complicated than in earlier eras as a large and growing proportion of women, worldwide, are making careers in the paid workforce. Yet the legacy of separation remains strong, lived out in powerful assumptions about what is "best" for men, women, and society. These assumptions result in tacit images of ideal workers, ideal parents, and ideal workplaces that create gender inequities.

Gendered Organizations in Social Context

The belief that men and women have distinct roles to play in society, based on gender differences, has a long history. In preindustrial societies, the differences between men's and women's musculature and reproductive organs largely explained and justified the division of labor within families. Men were the hunters, explorers, and warriors—with some notable female exceptions. The childbearing role kept women close to home and hearth. These differences translated into inferior status so that most, though not all, preindustrial families and societies were patriarchal, with women largely excluded from the public realm. Nonetheless, the division of labor between men and women was often not rigid. In preindustrial Western societies, for example, married women could not own property or claim economic return for their labor, but they often worked alongside their husbands and handled business affairs when necessary. Both parents worked long hours, and for both child rearing was a secondary activity, integrated into daily life.[1]

Social norms supporting separate gendered spheres became more clearly defined and more prescriptive in the context of industrialization in the Western world. As the importance of paid employment increased, the work of maintaining home life decreased in status. Indeed, the work of home life became increasingly invisible in economic models that conceptualized households as sites of consumption rather than production. At the same time, the role of motherhood gained in stature. The life situation of white, middle- and upper-class women was sentimentalized and, at least in theory, generalized to the entire population, resulting in what is often called the "cult of true womanhood." Raising a family became the *raison d'être* of the household, and nurturing the children—morally, psychologically, and intellectually, as well as physically—was an increasingly central part of an "ideal" mother's domestic responsibilities.[2] While these norms did not reflect the actual life situations of most of the population, male or female, they did reflect powerful cultural assumptions about work, family, and community.

In the aftermath of the Great Depression and World War II, middle-class men threw themselves into paid work and women into domesticity as never before, while family consumption drove an economic expansion. Family size increased with the postwar "baby boom," and a new popular literature on parenting, exemplified in the United States by the work of Dr. Benjamin Spock, exalted the parenting role of mothers.[3] At the same time, rapid suburbanization increased the disconnect between work and home life for men.[4] Again, these predominantly white, middle-class patterns did not fit the life situations of much of the population. They did, however, fit most of the men who made up the managerial ranks of large bureaucratic work organizations and who created the workplace structures, practices, and "rules for success" that continue to influence our understanding of organizational life.

Key assumptions about men, embedded in the concept of separate spheres, shaped these industrial-era organizational forms in powerful ways. One of the most critical was the assumption that paid work was a man's primary responsibility and constituted his main contribution to family life. Also important were related assumptions about male psychology: that men's sense of identity and self-worth derived mainly, if not exclusively, from employment and achievement in the world of paid work and that men were "naturally" competitive and individualistic, with all that this belief implied in terms of skills and character traits. These assumptions and images of idealized masculinity shaped key understandings, for example, about what it means to be competent at work. They also opened the door to an increasingly insatiable demand for commitment of time to work and laid the foundation for a work ethic that dictated acceptance of those demands.[5]

Shared by employers, employees, and society at large, gendered assumptions did not need to be stated or considered explicitly to have influence on organizational norms and practices. In fact, as Rosabeth Moss Kanter and others have observed, they were made at such a deep level of shared understanding that organizational design and dynamics could be, and have been, discussed and analyzed as entirely gender-neutral phenomena, both within organizations and in the literature about them.[6] Advancing equity at work requires a process of exploring, examining, and ultimately challenging these gendered assumptions.

Gendered Assumptions

Gendered assumptions influence the practice and structure of work in powerful but often invisible ways. Indeed, many of the implicit "rules for success" in today's workplace are closely aligned with traditional images of masculinity such as autonomy, assertiveness, competition, and heroic action. It makes sense that this would be so. The modern, industrialized workplace was created by and for a certain subset of men. So is it any wonder that many of the things we regard as normal or at least as having nothing to do with gender—things like meeting times, reporting structures, and even performance criteria—are a reflection of white, middle-class, masculine values and life situations? Though it may seem obvious in this context, the alignment of stereotypical masculinity with commonplace rules for success is far from obvious in practice. That is why our method of uncovering the assumptions that drive work behavior and then examining these assumptions using a "gender lens" is such a powerful opportunity for learning and change. People are often surprised to recognize that what they considered gender-neutral work practices are actually rooted in old, idealized images of masculinity, images that no longer reflect the values, experience, and life situations of most people, male or female, in today's workplace. In particular, our work has shown that the set of assumptions most directly linked to gender are assumptions about commitment and competence.

Commitment

In most workplaces, the definition of commitment remains rooted in a traditional concept of the ideal worker as someone for whom work is primary, time to spend at work is unlimited, and the demands of family, community, and personal life are secondary.[7] These are gendered assumptions. Their effect is that people who do not fit this description—for example, people who work part time or "job share"—often have jobs with severely constrained career opportunities. Although what constitutes a full-time job is arbitrary and has changed often over the years, the opportunities available for less than full-time work are often routine, repetitive jobs with little chance for advancement. It is often assumed that committed workers want or need to work full time. As one manager said to us, "Yes, I could break up that job into a couple of interesting part-time jobs, and it might even be better for the work if I did, but who would I get to take them? My best workers need full-time work." This line of reasoning becomes pernicious when applied in reverse, so that workers who *do* accept less than full-time work are assumed to be less committed or to have made a trade-off that makes them unreliable or less interested in challenging work. These assumptions limit the ability to think creatively about job design, a constraint that has obvious equity and effectiveness implications.

Time spent at work is another indicator of commitment that is gendered and affects both equity and effectiveness. For example, the timing and scheduling of meetings—whether formal or informal—can have a significant impact on both the amount of time people must work and the predictability of time commitments. When important meetings take place outside regular working hours, those who cannot attend are at a distinct disadvantage. At the same time, their absence has an impact on the quality and applicability of the decisions made at those meetings. As one female manager told her boss, "Sure, you can say it's OK that I don't attend because I have to pick up Jason at day care. But if you go on and hold the meeting anyway, what does that say about my contribution? And what do I do with decisions that are made that I may disagree with? It's not OK to tell me not to come. That is not an acceptable solution to the problem of having these meetings after work hours." Her manager was taken aback: he had thought of himself as a family-friendly manager; now he had to reconsider that view. Moreover, he had never considered how having meetings without all members present might be leading to inefficient or ineffective decisions.

"Doing whatever it takes" is also a way of demonstrating commitment that has gender equity as well as work effectiveness implications. While it might be considered a noble goal to have workers willing to do whatever it takes to get a job done, in practice this norm often translates into throwing time at problems. "Doing whatever it takes" is often a way of demonstrating that "time is no obstacle." For example, in one high-powered corporate staff group, every request for information or assignment from upper management was automatically assumed to be urgent, taking precedence over other tasks and justifying night and weekend work to get it done. People did not dare to ask questions about priorities because they feared singling themselves out as unwilling to "do whatever it takes." For employees in this work culture, what mattered was not just how effectively they performed their jobs but whether they were willing and able to perform on demand.

Organizational cultures that glorify employees who work as if they had no personal-life needs or responsibilities silence personal concerns and make it difficult to recognize or admit the costs of overwork. Interestingly, we have found this true not only in the high-powered corporate world but in some not-for-profit organizations as well. When commitment to a mission as important as alleviating poverty, for example, is measured by one's willingness to work long hours, travel extensively, and put work ahead of family or personal life, it is very difficult to acknowledge the burden this represents or to question the effectiveness of time-intensive work practices.

These issues are not just women's problems. Assumptions about commitment, which create these situations, also place constraints on men who want to participate actively in family and community life or who simply want to "have a life" outside of work. Many men speak poignantly about this dilemma — wanting and needing to have a different level of involvement in family and community life but feeling that to get ahead they *must* demonstrate that work comes first. These gendered expectations continue to place constraints on men's involvement in family life, even though there is a rising expectation that they will share the "second shift" with their partners.[8] Women, because they are still expected to shoulder the lion's share of that second shift, feel real constraints on their ability to succeed at work. These constraints result in missed opportunities for men to appreciate the joys and positive self-esteem that come from family involvement, for women to appreciate the joys and positive self-esteem that come from success at work, and for both work and family domains to reap the benefits of increased involvement by members of the "opposite" sex.

Competence

A second critical and even more knotty set of equity issues arises from assumptions about what it means—and what it takes—to be competent in the spheres of work and family life. The rules of success in one sphere are assumed to be at odds with the other, and the skills needed in one are assumed to be inappropriate or ill suited for the other. These assumptions are so ingrained that violating them is often used as a source of humor. Cartoon strips, movies, and commercials get our attention when they play on gender stereotypes, showing beleaguered men in aprons vacuuming or admonishing children to "wait till your mother gets home." While the spectacle of men flummoxed by domestic crises or women putting up curtains in the boardroom may be humorous, the implicit "truth" that is reinforced is far from funny: men and "masculinity" do not belong at home; women and "femininity" do not belong at work.

The fact that so many of the written and unwritten rules for how to demonstrate competence at work are closely aligned with idealized images of men and masculinity has several effects on gender equity. First, it makes it hard for women to play by the rules. Expectations of how a woman should behave create the classic double bind. If she does not display the required masculine characteristics, people see her as not "tough" enough or not "assertive" enough. But if she does, they may judge her as arrogant or even label her a "bitch." Women using the same tactics of success they have learned from male peers often hear, when it is time for promotion, that they are not in the pipeline because they are too abrasive, demanding, or as one woman was told, too much like a "man in a skirt."[9]

Of course, it is not only women who find it ineffective to work in the individualistic, authoritarian, self-promoting manner that is typically equated with competence in the workplace. We find in our individual, one-on-one interviews with men that many of them also find these norms troubling. And there is a growing literature offering an alternative picture of masculine strengths.[10] Nonetheless, a man can adopt the norms without calling into question his gender identity, but a woman cannot. So when displays of masculinity are conflated with what it takes to do the job, women are disadvantaged and constrained in how they work. As Virginia Valian notes, for men, masculinity and occupational success reinforce each other; for women, femininity and occupational success do not.[11]

Another equity problem that arises from masculine gendered norms of workplace competence is the devaluation of stereotypical feminine attributes, which people often lump together under the rubric of "interpersonal skills." In many organizations, for example, assumptions about competence and "real" work overemphasize technical capability and individual achievement while deemphasizing other equally important skills such as facilitating collective achievement, team building, or the ability to relate effectively to peers and external customers. Although most managers would say that both sets of skills are important to success, we find that when push comes to shove, it is the technical skills that are given precedence. The fact that people who have overly developed technical skills may be *deficient* in relational skills is often overlooked. Indeed, the lack of relational skills—especially in men—is rarely seen as a problem. Instead, it is often assumed that these skills will somehow be gained on the job.[12]

We see this pattern often. In a financial services department, for example, we noticed a difference between the attributes and abilities it took to get an analyst's job and the attributes and abilities it took to do the job well. In responding to questions about what it took to get ahead and be promoted into their high-level positions, analysts talked about quantitative and analytical skills as the basic requirements, with actuarial backgrounds being the most highly valued. Doing the job well, however, was not dependent on that set of skills alone. The ability to do good work was also dependent on getting good, timely, accurate data from other departments. People who really contributed to the overall effort were those who also had relational skills such as the ability to understand, empathize, and offer help. As one female analyst noted, "What you need to do is call down and instead of hassling people, ask them, 'What can I do to help you get the numbers?'—and then actually *doing* it. I've done things like get people lunch or even gone down there and crunched some numbers for them while they worked on pulling it all together." The willingness to do some lower-status work like getting someone lunch or crunching numbers, the ability to understand a situation and the pressures someone else was under and to create an appropriate response, were not skills seen as crucial to the job. More often, people who interacted with others in this way were regarded as especially "nice" or "thoughtful" rather than especially competent.[13] Seen as personal attributes rather than skills, these abilities were not mentioned in the job description, and people who had them—especially women—rarely thought of themselves as particularly qualified for the job and rarely thought of emphasizing these relational skills during the interviewing process. As a result, some people who might have applied did not, and those who were hired into the department often lacked the relational skills to be effective, despite their technical ability.

Summing Up

The common denominator in these examples of commitment and competence is the need to identify and reevaluate gendered assumptions about the attributes of the "ideal" worker, assumptions that are anchored in an implicit, strongly held belief in the separation between the occupational and the domestic spheres of life. These gendered assumptions undermine gender equity and make it difficult to achieve a fair allocation of opportunities for men and women to be involved and successful in work and in family life. But these assumptions also have another, equally serious consequence. Conflating idealized masculinity with what it takes to be the "ideal" worker often results in the persistence of dysfunctional, outdated, or ineffective practices that are routinized as normal and rarely questioned. Indeed, the fact that the resulting norms and practices are dysfunctional goes largely unnoticed in most workplaces. But being unnoticed does not lessen—and may in fact even strengthen—their impact in limiting not only equity but also workplace performance.

Relinking the Spheres: Integration, Not Balance

Gendered assumptions and stereotypes based in the separation of spheres constrain the choices of both women and men. Our vision of gender equity is to relax these social norms about separation so that men and women are free to experience these two parts of their lives as integrated rather than as separate domains that need to be "balanced." Integration would make it possible for both women and men to perform up to their capabilities and find satisfaction in both work and personal life, no matter how they allocate their time commitment between the two. To convey this goal, we speak of integrating work and personal life rather than balancing. This terminology expresses our belief in the need to diminish the separation between these two spheres of life in ways that will *change both*, rather than merely reallocating—or "balancing"—time between them as they currently exist.

A Vision of Integration

A world that allowed work–personal life integration would legitimate a diverse range of relationships to work. It would mean changing norms that assume the primacy of paid work and limit the career choices and opportunities of individuals who seek fulfillment through commitments in both work and personal life. It would also mean redefining implicit notions of commitment and competence to encourage and reward a more diverse set of skills and contributions in each sphere.

These potential outcomes of integration, although they sound simple enough, would have powerful effects on both work and personal-life domains. Breaking down the image of an "ideal" worker whose top priority is paid employment requires a complementary change in families, one that is rarely discussed or debated seriously. It also requires breaking down the image of an "ideal" caretaker as someone for whom paid work is unimportant or secondary. In other words, relaxing the separation between the two spheres would mean that our ideal images in each domain would change, as well as our tacit definition of competence and commitment in each. When displays of femininity are conflated with what it takes to do the job in the private sphere, men lose, just as women lose from masculine gendered workplace norms. With greater integration, the appropriateness of behavior would no longer be linked to idealized gender images but rather to the requirements of the job and the tasks at hand.

The full range of actual changes in "ideal practice" in each sphere that might result from this kind of linking can only be imagined. What would families and communities look like if caretaking norms valued involvement in and skills from the public domain of paid work? What would our workplaces look like if the norms in paid work expanded to include family and community involvement and skills derived from activities in those realms? What would our very notions of "masculinity" and "femininity" be if these images were not tied to the gendered division of labor? Answering these questions is not something that can be accomplished by sitting in an ivory tower of theory and abstract reasoning. It requires action research: working on the ground, with people who have been given the power and opportunity to think "out of the box" about their work in each sphere and about how the skills developed in one can be used—with appropriate effect—in the other.

Although integration requires that images of excellence in both spheres change, our action research focuses on identifying and making small, concrete doable changes (something we call "small wins")[14] in the public sphere of paid work. We do this because we believe that in today's global economy, the workplace offers the most potential—and is the ripest—for change. New ideas about leadership, teams, and collaboration highlight the need for relational skills traditionally associated with the personal domain and provide an opportunity to demonstrate the strategic benefits of integrating rather than separating the two spheres.[15] In addition, the urgency to start with the workplace to make this type of change is great. The Western model of individual success—with its emphasis on paid work as one's primary source of self-esteem—is being exported to the rest of the world at an alarming pace.

Insufficiency of Individual Accommodations

Although we have described underlying gendered assumptions about work, ideal workers, and images of success as society-level phenomena, it is important to realize that most people do not experience them as such. On the contrary, most of us experience them not as social norms at all but as individual choices. As one engineer said regarding commitment, "It's not a problem if you want to put work first. And it's not a problem if you want to put family first. It's only a problem when you care about both." When that problem arises, people find themselves largely on their own in dealing with it.

Individual solutions to meet these demands may help people balance, but they have little effect on their ability to integrate work and personal life. For example, many organizations rely on managers to be sensitive to work–personal life conflicts when employees speak up. Many others have turned to employee assistance programs (EAPs) that help working men and women identify and address both work and personal-life problems through individualized counseling and information services. Such accommodations, while important, have little effect on the underlying work culture. Managers who believe that their best workers are those who are willing and able to spend unlimited time at work are unlikely to promote or give their most challenging new projects to people who have asked for work accommodations. The result is that people feel they have to choose. In fact, the little-recognized but powerful cumulative effect of these individual solutions is to reinforce the societal dictum about individual choice: Which is more important to you, work or personal life? Indeed, we hear all the time that it is impossible for anyone—especially women—to "have it all." Moving beyond balance to integration offers something different, a more systemic approach that *challenges* gendered concepts of commitment and competence rather than accepting them as gender-neutral standards that individuals can "choose" to accept.

Conclusion

Our vision of gender equity means undoing the separation between the private and public spheres that characterizes the Western industrial world. Such a transformation goes against everything we have been taught to think and feel. It means breaking down the image of an ideal worker as someone who conforms to stereotypical masculine norms in terms of values, attributes, and life situation. More specifically, it means breaking down the image of an ideal worker as someone whose only priority is the job and at the same time breaking down the image of the ideal caretaker as someone whose life is given to care but whose contribution is assumed to be "natural" and thus not given equal social or economic value.

Our experience so far is in the workplace. There we have found that work groups that uncover and examine gendered assumptions about their work find the process energizing and exciting. Looking at the work itself, rather than at policies, unleashes a sense of possibility and creativity. The result is a plethora of ideas for changes in work practices that would be good for the work and good for gender equity and work–personal life integration.

Pursuing equity in gendered organizations through these types of work practice changes, however, is not simple. It requires a certain kind of process. In Part Two, we describe the basic elements of this process and the method we have used to identify gendered assumptions, design work practice changes, and implement those changes to meet the Dual Agenda. But first, we continue the discussion of integration with a closer examination of the Dual Agenda concept.

CHAPTER 3

Linking Equity and Organizational Effectiveness: The Dual Agenda

When we examine the gendered aspects of organizational life, the negative implications for individuals who do not fit the masculine image of excellence are clear. Their lives are stressed, and it is difficult, if not impossible, for them to perform up to their full potential. What has become increasingly evident in our research is that these same conditions also undermine organizational effectiveness, which leads, as already indicated, to a key finding: *making changes in work practices that increase gender equity can also increase workplace performance and organizational effectiveness.* In other words, we have found that expecting all good workers to be like post–World War II white, Western, middle-class men, in their life situations and characteristics, is not only a problem for women's career advancement but is also a problem for the work of the organization itself, preventing everyone—men and women alike—from working in the most effective ways to achieve workplace goals. This intersection of equity and effectiveness is the basis for the Dual Agenda.

The Dual Agenda

The concept of the Dual Agenda runs counter to conventional wisdom at both ends of the spectrum. People who are primarily committed to increasing gender equity or to making work organizations more "family-friendly" believe deeply that these are goals worth pursuing for their own sake, regardless of the impact on performance. Managers, whose charge is to sustain or improve performance, often agree that these issues require attention, but their goal is to minimize the amount of time, money, and energy such personal (or personnel) issues divert from the primary concerns of the organization.[1] The common element in these perspectives is the assumption that accommodating those who do not fit the currently accepted employee mold represents a cost, not an investment. Our view is quite different. Based on a growing body of evidence, our belief is that there need not be a trade-off: organizations can serve their own ends *and* those of their employees by addressing these issues.[2]

How can this happen? By inviting employees to bring their personal concerns to bear when looking critically at work practices, one taps tremendous reserves of energy and motivation. People want in any case to be effective in their work, but incorporating a personal payoff into the goals of organizational change provides a powerful added incentive for engagement.

Unexpected Connections

We saw this effect vividly in a sales and service group that was consistently underperforming in both sales and customer satisfaction. It was clear that many of the problems stemmed from lack of communication between sales and service as well as from lack of appreciation of how the strains and stresses in each function were exacerbated by the other. For example, service technicians felt that the sales tendency to promise customers unrealistic levels of service was the source of much of the stress and unpredictability in their jobs. Sales felt that the lack of responsiveness of service reps resulted in the loss of valuable repeat customers. Cross-functional teams to increase communication and understanding had been tried in the past with little success. When we arrived on the scene, sales and service were still struggling separately with their own work and personal-life concerns: long hours for sales personnel; unpredictability for service reps who had to respond to calls at all hours. Jointly, we put together a new cross-functional pilot team that over a period of nine months was able to turn the situation around.

What made this attempt different was the additional goal of work–personal life integration. Why? Because in any new structure, such as a cross-functional team, there are bound to be problems, unforeseen rough spots, and an initial time investment in doing things differently. Adding and legitimating the goal of work–personal life integration gives people the energy and enthusiasm for working through the rough spots. As one member of the team said, "We are going to *make* this work.

Because if it works, I might actually have a life!" With this level of commitment to the change, members found opportunities to share information and support each other in ways that both improved performance and ameliorated work–personal life conflicts. In the process, they overcame entrenched attitudes of mutual mistrust and disrespect.

In this case and in many others in diverse work settings, we have observed the phenomenon of Dual Agenda initiatives achieving breakthroughs in solving seemingly intractable organizational problems. In every instance, motivating work groups to engage in work redesign by legitimating personal as well as performance issues was a key success factor.

Making this unexpected connection also confers another critical advantage. Repeatedly, our research has shown that linking personal and organizational issues is a source of insight and creativity in both areas. To get at these links, we ask questions such as "What does it take to be seen as competent (or committed) around here?" and "What is it about your work that creates difficulty for your personal life?" Such questions bring out work-related problems that people usually feel they must wrestle with on their own or simply endure. And when we probe more deeply for the causes of these problems, we begin to surface some of the gendered cultural assumptions that dictate how work is done or how individual contributions are evaluated. This, in turn, leads to a more systemic view and potentially more productive solutions to problems.

The case of a nonprofit agricultural research institute illustrates this process.[3] Concerned by the underrepresentation of women in the professional and managerial ranks of the organization, the director brought in an outside team to help work on gender equity issues. The team interviewed roughly one-fourth of the staff individually, exploring the institute's daily tasks and schedules, formal and informal expectations, decision-making and reward systems, and workload. The goal was to understand the institute's work practice norms, the underlying assumptions that accounted for these norms, and the differences in how men and women experienced them.

What emerged was the image of a work culture rooted in a set of assumptions about heroic individualism. Work practices and rewards, as well as formal and informal criteria for excellence, reflected an implicit belief that the institute's success and reputation depended on attracting, retaining, and supporting intellectual "stars." These intellectual giants were expected to produce high-quality strategic research that would be published in leading academic journals. In the past, this ethic of academic individualism had served the institute well. The larger environment, however, had changed in recent years. Policymakers around the world were less interested in academically oriented research produced by a few leading lights. They wanted information and understanding focused on practical policy concerns and developed more collaboratively, both with client countries and across a range of academic disciplines. As a result, the institute's donors had begun to insist on greater accountability and to make grants on a project-by-project rather than a sustaining basis. The institute's leadership realigned its strategic priorities in response to these changes. But, the Dual Agenda team found, the culture of individualism remained strong, even though it was in conflict with the new strategic direction.

Assumptions about the importance of academic "stars" continued to govern formal and informal systems of recognition and evaluation, favoring publication in elite journals above all other criteria for success. Funding for research support flowed primarily to those who succeeded by this standard. Hence contributions of the sorts the institute as a whole needed to succeed in the new environment—such as outreach and collaboration in client countries—tended to go unrecognized. People who considered such initiatives important and devoted time to them still had to publish in order to fulfill the job requirements and advance their careers and to do so with limited research support. Collaborative projects within the institute, although an important part of the new strategy, did not replace the tacit requirement for individual research but simply added to it. For most people, collaborative and individual work were placed in direct conflict. The additional meetings and communication required by the new strategy pushed the individual work of research analysis and writing outside regular work hours. Given the underlying culture, the result was that collaborative work was stalled and people in the organization felt plagued by an excessive workload.

It was the women in the organization who experienced these problems most acutely. The assumption that much of the research work could be done outside the regular workday was an added burden for those whose ability to work in off hours was constrained by family responsibilities. Also, women occupied many of the support positions that enabled the "individual" achievement of the academic stars, and they were often asked to take on much of the outreach and collaborative work. But women were not the only ones caught up in this dynamic. It also affected men from developing countries who, because they did not have the same resources and networks of support, found the new demands hard to meet. Nowhere was there recognition of the systemic forces leading to these inequitable results. Instead, people felt they had to wrestle with the overload on their own, in keeping with the individualistic ethos of the organization, where working long hours was simply what a committed professional was expected to do.

Though women initially highlighted these issues, in the long run, everyone stood to gain from addressing them. A series of roundtable discussions with the entire staff produced more than ninety suggestions for changes in work practices. No one experiment held the key in this case. But over a period of years, new attitudes, in particular toward the use and value of time, took hold as more and more people began to push back on unrealistic expectations. Eventually, the institute's managers found ways of formally acknowledging time spent on building and nurturing relationships, and they agreed to structure such use of time into research proposals and work plans—a suggestion they had originally resisted on the grounds that productivity, quality, and funding might suffer.

These steps, as well as others aimed at developing and supporting collaborative skills and making the system of securing research funding more fair, were changes the institute's leaders had already identified as critical for a realignment of its strategic priorities. But they had not connected the needed changes to the workload, stress, and gender inequity issues that plagued the institute. The connection—and the energy to deal creatively with the kinds of cultural change needed—emerged only when people began to understand the power and resiliency of the culture of individualism and were able to think about ways to address the issues systemically rather than expecting people to deal with them on their own.

These two examples demonstrate some key findings of our Dual Agenda research: gendered assumptions in work cultures not only undermine equity but often also undermine the changes organizations want and need to make in order to function effectively in an increasingly complex and challenging environment. Even in cases where the changes in strategic direction have already been identified, old, deeply embedded, taken for granted assumptions continue to influence concrete work practices. These work practices are amazingly resilient—a resiliency that we believe is rooted in their connection to gender identity, gender expectations, and gender roles. Examining work through a gender lens lays bare these gendered assumptions, as well as the specific, concrete everyday work practices that are governed by them. In turn, these work practices serve as leverage points for action. Identifying them creates opportunities to devise changes that would advance both equity and workplace effectiveness.

Leverage Points for Action

In our engagement with these issues over many years with a number of different organizations, we have learned that the key points of intersection between equity and effectiveness reside in two key areas. In Chapter Two, we identified these, generally, as commitment and competence. We have found that when we ask people to reflect on issues of competence and commitment, they mention work practice norms that offer opportunities for Dual Agenda change. These norms cluster in four categories (see Exhibit 3.1).

The Use and Politics of Time.   How employees use their time at work and how that use is interpreted—what we call the politics of time—relate directly to organizational effectiveness, as evidenced by the extensive management literature on time-based competition. Working smarter, faster, and more efficiently is a legitimate and often a pressing goal in all types of work settings. Time is also a critical equity issue for people who have significant commitments outside of work. For them, work time is not infinitely expandable, nor are all times of the day equally available for work. Thus the use and politics of time are issues for all who wish to have challenging, meaningful work and still "have a life."

When we look at patterns around the use of time through a gender lens, we often find work practices that are based on the gendered assumption that the ideal worker is willing and able to devote as much time to work as the work seems to demand. This ideal has supported the continual encroachment of work responsibilities into personal time by making the amount of time spent working, and often simply physical presence at work, the main measure of commitment to the job. As one engineering manager said to us, "I know who my best workers are—they are the guys who don't know enough to go home at night." This attitude that the best employee is the one who spends the most time at work has helped foster the belief that work output is directly, and linearly, related to the amount of time spent on work—an idea that reinforces the norms surrounding long work hours and, in turn, reinforces the work practices that unwittingly lead to the *need* to spend these long hours at work.

This dynamic was evident in a high-tech marketing team that operated in a continual crisis mode.[4] The team had developed norms around new-client opportunities that treated each as a crisis, often working around the clock to deliver a proposal and presentation. When other workers arrived in the morning to find the marketing team still there, the team often received a round of applause for extraordinary effort. Of course, team members' personal lives suffered from this arrangement. In fact, in an indirect

Exhibit 3.1. A Checklist of Work Practices and Norms That Have Equity and Effectiveness Implications.

The Use and Politics of Time

- When and where are meetings held?

- What are the norms of scheduling, deadlines, and due dates?

- What time of day is most valuable and why?

- Who has autonomy over time spent at work? Who does not?

- Are norms in line with the requirements of the job?

Images of Top Performance

- What behavior is reinforced or rewarded?

- Is there a difference in the type of behavior rewarded in the formal as opposed to the informal process?

- What behavior demonstrates competence?

- Where are the opportunities to demonstrate competence?

- What does it take to be seen as a potential leader?

- How does one earn the respect of colleagues?

- Is there a difference in how one earns the respect of colleagues as opposed to the respect of supervisors?

Beliefs About Hierarchy and Control

- What are the assumed requirements of a leadership job?

- Who are the leadership role models?

- What are their personal life situations?

- To what degree is this in line with the goal or mission of the organization?

Definitions of "Real" Work

- What behavior or output is considered valuable?

- What behavior is considered connected to the organization's goal or mission?

- What is the tacit definition of output?
- How is output measured?
- In group meetings, who speaks? Who listens?
- What interaction or conversational style is considered "normal"?
- What interaction or conversational style is considered "deviant"?
- How, when, and where are decisions made?

way, this personal-life cost was the clearest demonstration of their commitment. However, when we looked more carefully at the patterns of work affected by these norms, we found a number of hidden business costs, not only to the quality of the projects but also to the overall effort of the firm. For example, teams that had pulled "all-nighters" in preparation for a client presentation were often able, through sheer adrenaline, to make it through the client meeting successfully. After the meeting, they often went out for a celebratory lunch and then home for much needed rest and a late—or nonexistent—arrival the next day. What was hidden in this pattern was that during the several days of recovery following their all-nighters, other team members often had to put their own work on hold, delaying the planning cycle for the next client presentation and setting up a repeat of the need for future all-nighters.

Because of beliefs that time is an indicator of quality and commitment, the costs to the overall work of the department went largely unnoticed. Instead, the group's manager celebrated each completed proposal as a success and praised the team for its commitment to getting the job done. There was no incentive, in this environment, for the team to change this pattern by anticipating problems, for example, and planning ahead. Nor was it likely that individual team members would feel comfortable questioning the costs of this behavior on personal grounds. Instead, this dysfunctional work practice remained firmly entrenched, continuously reinforced by the cycle of congratulations and the lack of recognition of the subsequent loss of productive time.

There are many other examples of how the politics of time creates inequities. In one situation, time away from work during the middle of the day—to exercise or take a long lunch—did not carry the same negative career consequences as time away in the early morning or late in the day. In another, engineers held meetings, which they considered "voluntary" project status reports, every morning at 7:00 A.M. to discuss problems and issues arising in their areas. In yet another, "stretch" schedules—schedules so ambitious as to be virtually impossible to adhere to—created a work mode of continuous crisis. Such schedules, based on an implicit belief that people work better when they are under pressure, result in demands for weekend and late evening work. And in another situation, a work group made decisions during the day with everyone present only to see them reversed as the result of after-hours discussions between the group leader and the boss. Asking questions about the politics of time brings to the surface many routine and rarely questioned work practices that have negative consequences for equity and effectiveness. It is a good way to identify opportunities for Dual Agenda change.

Images of Top Performance.   Another set of norms that indicates leverage points for action are practices that people undertake to meet tacit images of leadership, excellence, or top performance. Masculine images and other gendered assumptions about what good work behavior "looks like" influence how people work and interact and what characteristics they emphasize. In an environment that values technical contributions and heroic problem solving over all else, people vie for time in meetings to demonstrate their command of the details of a problem, even if the problem is not one the group itself can or even should be solving. In an environment that values individual rather than collective know-how, people keep bits of knowledge to themselves, using information as power—a way to advance their careers rather than advance the work. In an environment that values competitiveness and pits individuals against each other so that the "cream will rise to the top," people work to undermine rather than support one another's efforts. These work practices are problematic for women because they are so aligned with traditional notions of masculinity that women who demonstrate them are often shunned or negatively labeled. Nor is it only women who suffer. These individualistic masculine norms and the competitiveness they foster can undermine an organization's efforts to meet the emerging demands of work.

Increasing complexity of the external environment and incessant pressure to accomplish more with the same or fewer resources are part of twenty-first-century reality in the nonprofit as well as the for-profit sector. Most organizations recognize the need for more collaborative ways of working to meet these challenges, for cooperation and a spirit of inquiry and learning across functions, up and down hierarchies, with customers and suppliers, and within work groups and teams. Yet as in the case of the agricultural research institute described earlier, organizations that recognize the strategic necessity of working more cooperatively must still confront the reality of entrenched attitudes and patterns that support and reward just the opposite. Naming and holding up to scrutiny the negative consequences of these norms, still embedded in an outdated image of competence, yield many leverage points for action.

For example, in a core department of a large manufacturing company, one way of demonstrating competence was always to have the answer to anything that came up. This reliance on individual knowledge led to dysfunctional norms about not asking questions, which had negative consequences not only for individuals but for the business as well. The norm of not asking clarifying questions meant that people had to work on multiple scenarios when only one or two were actually needed or to create reports with sophisticated charts when only "back of the envelope" preliminary ideas were called for. Asking questions that would establish boundaries was taboo because people thought that asking questions might signal that they were less competent and less committed than they were expected to be.

As with all Dual Agenda issues, looking at this situation through a gender lens helped identify both the equity and effectiveness consequences. We found, first, that the women in this industry dominated by men had their competence questioned because they did not fit the image people had of top performers, since almost all previous top workers were men. This immediate disadvantage made it even more difficult for women to ask clarifying questions. By asking for more information, they would be violating still another norm, which would reinforce their "deviance." Even more problematic, if their asking questions was interpreted as reflecting an unwillingness to put in time, they feared being seen as "mommy track" candidates rather than "fast track." But the business implications of the norm were also serious. Not asking clarifying questions resulted in a tendency to overdo work and also increased the need for frequent redos. These time-wasting patterns caused unnecessary overtime and workload stress, which in turn made it difficult to recruit people—both men and women—into a group renowned for its long hours.

This dysfunctional norm had a worthy goal: to demonstrate competence and commitment. But it also had these unintended negative consequences. Once the group identified them, it was relatively easy to come up with a solution to the problem. It designed an information form with several simple parameters that had to accompany all requests. Since this took the onus off individuals to ask questions, the career consequences of obtaining the information needed for a job were diminished. Men, women, *and* the organization reaped the benefit.

Beliefs About Hierarchy and Control. Organizations embrace empowerment and self-management as goals for the same reasons they embrace cooperation: because these modes of working hold promise for enabling people to be more flexible and productive in complex environments. Yet encouraging employees to take control of their work goes against one of the most deeply engrained gendered assumptions, that organizations run best when the people in charge are good at giving direction and subordinates are good at taking direction and acting on it. This central, patriarchal premise of managerial hierarchy makes it extremely difficult for organizations and individual managers to abandon the command-and-control style of leadership. At the same time, the rigid and tightly controlled work environment that top-down management tends to create makes it extremely difficult for employees to resolve conflicts between work and personal life. Where they are present, beliefs about hierarchy and control emerge clearly as issues for Dual Agenda projects.

Here is an example of how this assumption can lead to dysfunctional norms and practices. Management at one customer administration site was trying to introduce self-managed teams. However, their effort to produce multiskilled, self-directed work groups was falling short of expectations because the supervisors of these teams had hierarchical assumptions that ended up undermining teamwork. For example, believing that they needed to be there whenever their workers were on site, supervisors were reluctant to approve proposals for flexible hours that would extend the workday. They treated requests for flexible work arrangements in individual, one-off negotiations and granted only a limited number, which then led to charges of favoritism and unfairness. It also led to much unscheduled absenteeism as employees devised their own individual solutions to the problem of inflexible work hours.

Teamwork in such an environment obviously suffered; so did the teams' ability to respond to changing market conditions. Once the head of the division understood these connections, he mandated a three-month experiment that allowed employees to decide their own schedules as long as the work got done. This change shifted control over schedules from supervisors to the work groups. Employees gained the ability to integrate work and personal life more effectively and had to take greater responsibility for performance. Management got the empowered teams it wanted, with the added benefits of sharply reduced absenteeism and increased customer satisfaction because the flexible schedules expanded the hours of operation at both ends of the day, making it easier to meet the needs of customers in the new global environment.

Definitions of "Real" Work.   Another set of leverage points for action emerges from the way an organization classifies the importance of tasks. Despite an emphasis on teamwork, most organizations define certain aspects of work as more central than others. This hierarchy of tasks subtly but powerfully influences work practices and patterns of interaction between groups. Implicit divisions between what is considered vitally important work—or "real" work—that contributes to the mission and work that is seen as support work often lead to dysfunctional work practices with negative consequences for equity as well as effectiveness. Sometimes it is scientists who are seen as doing the most valuable work in the organization, sometimes it is engineers, sometimes faculty members, sometimes marketing or sales personnel. In all cases, the belief that the "real" work of the organization is done by a subset of people with special skills or training results in many other people feeling that their work is invisible in the final product. This kind of division often leads to resentment or competition between groups and to a number of work practices that people identify as ineffective time wasters.

For example, in one organization we worked with, there was a clear premium on the "hands-on" work of scientists who generated the final product for the customer. The valuing of this concrete product was so extreme that people involved in anything that could be considered support work found their work and contribution routinely dismissed or devalued. This was true not only for typical support positions, such as research assistants and secretarial staff, but also for more prestigious support functions from departments like Biotechnology (which was not the core scientific discipline of this organization) and Publications. In principle, there was recognition that all output was the result of organizationwide team effort, and there was much talk, especially from top management, about how success was a group, not an individual, product. The organization was moving to a team-based structure, which it considered imperative for addressing the complex, cross-functional issues it was facing. But in its everyday operations, support contributions were routinely treated as less important.

This pattern created a number of practices that detracted from gender equity. First, since women tended to be clustered in the support positions, their contributions were undervalued. Second, when asked, many women said that the real value they added to projects—even going beyond their technical expertise in some instances—was something they called the "glue" work, or "managing the white space" in a project. This work, like connecting people, smoothing difficulties, facilitating teamwork, or teaching others new skills, was critical to success but tended to be done behind the scenes and "off-line." As a result, it was largely invisible. There also was an informal norm in this organization of individuals taking sole credit for projects even when others had contributed to them or "saved" them from major catastrophes. In fact, this norm was so strong that many women reported having been given advice by mentors to avoid these kinds of activities in favor of other, more visible contributions. Such advice and tacit knowledge of what it takes to get ahead in this workplace undermined the probability that all tasks necessary for success were being handled by competent personnel.

Once the group understood the situation in this way, it came up with a concrete problem to solve: how to make critically important but invisible work more visible. This led to some interesting discussions and some important discoveries. One was the realization that this was not just a women's issue and that many men also felt that their contributions were invisible. So together they recommended to top management that it institute an organizationwide multisource evaluation system (something that is often called 360-degree feedback) that would allow peers and direct reports to give input on the quality of each person's work performance. When management agreed, the group contributed further by working on the performance criteria to be incorporated into the evaluation tool, to ensure that it included all the activities people considered invisible work. When we checked back with this organization several years later, both men and women were feeling that there had been a real change in the behaviors and concrete practices that were encouraged and rewarded. Relational competence was no longer invisible. Management felt that the new system was a key element in its move to a team-based organization—in reality, not just in words—and women, in particular, felt that there was a stronger and more accurate assessment of their contributions to the organization.[5]

Thus Dual Agenda work, which uncovers underlying assumptions and the gendered norms and practices that are embedded in them, points to areas of the work situation that are leverage points for action. The process of identifying specific constructive changes in work practices is an exciting, energizing opportunity to learn about the work culture and begin to envision the possibilities and benefits of doing things differently. Implementing these changes in a way that keeps both equity and effectiveness issues on the table, however, is a challenging process.

Dual Agenda Changes: The Importance of Keeping the Connection

The link between equity and effectiveness—between effective work practices and equitable work arrangements—sounds simple and straightforward. It is not. Focusing on multiple goals in a change process is always difficult, but in this case it is often the most challenging part of implementing project ideas. This connection runs so counter to expectations and assumptions about organizational life and business success that there is a built-in resistance to working on the issues together. Countless occasions arise to disconnect them and emphasize only one-half of the Dual Agenda. When this happens, the overall goal suffers and the project itself flounders.

One of our surprises has been that there are equally powerful forces for disconnection on each side of the Dual Agenda. Our assumption going into these projects was that there would be a tendency to focus on the effectiveness outcomes at the expense of equity goals. We cautioned managers and were vigilant ourselves about making sure that when a project was implemented, it did not lose its equity goals—or as we came to say, did not "lose gender." However, we found that this was not the only problem. It was often difficult to keep the work and the effectiveness goals in the project. The fact is that *both* parts of the agenda must be considered whenever implementation issues arise. When something in the implementation process is not working well, both sets of goals must be examined, both must inform whatever changes need to be made, and both must be covered by the criteria for judging success. And although there are dangers for the project in whichever side of the Dual Agenda is dropped, the effects and consequences are different, as the following examples suggest.

Dropping Equity

One example of dropping equity comes from a manufacturing organization that was deeply concerned about gender equity. Women accounted for a large percentage of shop-floor workers, but few were in supervisory or team leader positions. Analysis of the situation traced it back to gendered assumptions about competence and good management. More specifically, here, too, there was a disconnect between the attributes it took to *get* the job and those it took to *do* the job. Although many women had demonstrated the relational skills necessary to do the job of team leadership, when it came time for promotions to be made, these skills were regarded not as qualifications but as some nice "extras" that were not essential to leadership performance.

The action research team found traces of these assumptions in the job description for the position. It was easy to see that the attributes required for the position—discipline, authority, and constant availability—would draw men to the job and discourage women, who might question whether they had the requisite capabilities. It was also easy to see that given the work supervisors actually did day to day—such as building team collaboration, dealing with conflicts, and acting as liaison with other teams and other units of the company—the organization's criteria for promotion into supervisory positions were not the most appropriate for the job. Indeed, they may have accounted for some of the work problems it was experiencing with coordination and collaboration among work teams.

The pilot intervention on the basis of these insights was to define more explicitly a system of team management based on liaison building, collaboration, and self-management. The group assumed that putting these new requirements in writing would achieve the desired changes. Relational skills that many women possessed would be valued more highly, women would therefore be more likely to put their names into the hat when team leader selection was discussed, and over a period of time the issues of both equity and effectiveness would be well served. What happened was a different story.

As the unit moved to self-managed teams, old norms and attitudes reasserted themselves in interesting ways. People held on to the part of the analysis that surfaced the need for relational skills. But they lost sight of the part that described how those skills were "disappeared" as skills when women demonstrated them, by characterizing, for example, the women as "nice" or "thoughtful" rather than as "effective" or "demonstrating leadership." When only men's names appeared on the lists of possible team leader candidates, no one asked what systemic factors might be responsible. Instead, managers assumed that women were still not interested in the position. As a result, they gave the jobs to men who had relational skills, even if these skills were not as advanced as many the women had demonstrated. Within a few months, old norms of behavior reasserted themselves, and team leaders were exerting control over the groups in ways that undermined rather than reinforced interdependence and teamwork.[6]

Dropping Effectiveness

In the corporate accounting department of a large manufacturing firm, workload pressure was extreme. Everyone struggled with the time requirements of the work, which included major crunch times and slack periods interspersed with some tasks having horrendously tight deadlines and some with unpredictable time requirements. For example, because the department was responsible for assessing the financial implications of strategic decisions, employees were often called in at the eleventh hour to run an additional scenario or adjust an economic indicator based on new information. In addition to this unpredictable source of overtime work, there were natural peaks and valleys in the reporting cycle that people could prepare for in their personal lives. As one member said, "My family knows that the end of the reporting cycle means I won't be home in the evenings. It's OK; we have adjusted our life to accommodate that." The real personal-life stress came in not being able to smooth out these rough times with a lessening of work demands during off times. People noted that in looking ahead, they could predict times of slack in their work schedules when they would not be needed at night. But because of work norms that equated time at work with commitment, they did not feel they could take time off to attend to personal-life concerns even during slack times.

The group saw this as a leverage point for change, because everyone, managers included, believed that having people schedule compensatory time off in small chunks during the down times would help both the effectiveness of the work and people's ability to integrate work with personal life. For example, in the discussions with one work group, people envisioned times when they knew they would be working at night because the top management team was meeting late in the day and would be likely to send down requests for additional information to be available first thing in the morning. They thought that if they had the freedom to plan to arrive later that morning or to take off time in the middle of the day to attend a school function or get to the dry cleaner, it would ease their work–personal life stress immensely and actually benefit the work by freeing them to spend the hours necessary at night with renewed energy and less resentment.

After many brainstorming sessions, one team designed a pilot project it thought might achieve those results. Called Coordinated Work Schedules, this plan aimed to create flexibility that fit the unpredictable nature of the unit's work as well as the natural peaks and valleys of the financial reporting cycle. The unit put up a board in the office that listed the five different work groups and the people within each area. When people were going to "flex," they put up the times they would be out of the office so that everyone—managers and co-workers alike—would be aware of their schedules. Concerned that some workers might abuse the system, the team came up with guidelines that differentiated this informal flexibility from existing formal policies regarding vacation and compensatory time. It also devised a way for individuals to challenge each other if it seemed that things were getting out of balance. The purpose was to take the onus off managers to patrol the initiative and to place the responsibility on work group members themselves.

We handed the plan for these changes off to the unit, then returned eight months later for a follow-up evaluation. We found that Coordinated Work Schedules had operated very well for a number of months following their implementation. Nearly everyone in the unit took advantage of the flexibility—including managers, if only rarely. Use of the flextime benefit was situational: people "flexed" in slack times and remained available for crunch times, which enabled employees to feel that there was no stigma attached to doing so. The unit reduced its overtime, and people reported feeling less stressed, more energized at work, relieved at not having to make special requests to managers in order to attend to personal business, and more in control of their work and personal lives.

Eventually, though, the flextime benefit became separated from work considerations. Some people began to treat flexibility more as an entitlement, like vacation time, paying less attention to the impact on others and on the work unit as a whole. The mechanism for preventing this kind of abuse broke down. Lacking experience and skills in conflict management, co-workers avoided challenging each other over real or perceived abuses and instead went to managers to complain. Managers worried that the work might be suffering but felt that they could not raise these concerns without being seen as "non-family-friendly." In addition, the head of the unit, pleased with the initial gains in effectiveness of the work and enjoying some of the benefits of "flexing" himself, had issued an edict that people could extend the flexing to full days and that once a day off was put up on the board and the worker had made plans, those plans should not be interrupted except in the severest of emergencies. That made it much more difficult to reassert the effectiveness goal of the experiment.

Subsequently, a number of new people joined the unit, including some managers who were not aware of the spirit and intention of the pilot. They did not participate, and they resented having to deal with the team issues and administrative hassles it involved. When they began to express negative reactions to people who flexed, people using the plan became concerned for their careers. By the time we returned to assess the situation, no one was using Coordinated Work Schedules as originally planned. By dropping effectiveness and focusing only on personal-life benefits, the organization achieved neither.

These two cases illustrate the greatest challenge in Dual Agenda projects: maintaining focus on *both* parts of the agenda throughout. In our experience, only the two objectives together have the power to loosen the grip of gendered assumptions in organizational cultures. Yet there is always intense pressure to drop one or the other, precisely because connecting them runs so counter to conventional wisdom. Thus the challenge of holding the dual focus is always there and presents itself at every step of a Dual Agenda project. The method we have evolved, Collaborative Interactive Action Research (CIAR), has taken its present form partly in response to this challenge.

The Dual Agenda and CIAR

The Dual-Agenda mission is embedded in every step of our organizational change method. In individual and group interviews, we ask about both sets of issues—the effectiveness of work practices and their impact on employees' lives. We look for opportunities to make people aware of the connection between the two, and we continually challenge the assumption that there is none. Seizing those opportunities in what we call micro-interventions or "push-backs" has become an integral part of CIAR. In our analysis of the data, we look for structures and practices that affect both organizational effectiveness and equity. Using the gender lens in this way provides fresh perspective on familiar organizational issues.

The action steps in CIAR have a specific character because of these dual objectives. When we collaborate in planning interventions, we are careful to ensure that the group considers both sides of the Dual Agenda and makes challenging gendered assumptions an explicit part of experimental changes. In designing changes, we look at both concerns and push the design team to think creatively about both kinds of outcomes. For example, on equity indicators of successful change, we might ask, "Have long hours abated?" "Are more women applying, accepting, and succeeding?" And on measures of performance and quality, we might ask, "Is the organization more effective, with less overtime, fewer crises, more collaboration?"

The Dual Agenda has shaped CIAR on a more fundamental level as well—it has pushed us to develop a methodology that *itself* challenges the gendered assumptions we are trying to surface and dislodge in organizations. More specifically, our method incorporates important elements of a relational model of learning, expressed in the concepts of fluid expertise and mutuality.[7] It is a mode of working together that honors the skills and knowledge that each party brings to the collaboration and allows expertise to shift from one to another depending on the needs of the situation. Hence the emphasis on a particular type of collaboration and interaction and on the particular meaning we give to the dynamic of working together and influencing each other that is captured in those terms. We believe, in short, that this method is inseparable from the mission it is designed to serve.

Conclusion

Linking gender equity to the goal of increasing organizational effectiveness makes an unexpected connection. These objectives seem adversarial because they are deeply embedded in the separation of spheres—the public sphere of paid work and the private sphere of personal life. Our research indicates that making this connection, particularly at the level of work practices, can produce significant improvements in people's lives and in workplace performance. Making these changes involves uncovering and examining gendered assumptions, also rooted in the separation of spheres, that underlie the organization of work. The process of defining these assumptions and identifying the ways that they shape particular work practices indicates leverage points for change. The results can be surprising and powerful, but they are challenging to sustain, because holding on to both parts of the Dual Agenda—maintaining that unexpected connection—is difficult.

In Part Two, we present a method—Collaborative Interactive Action Research (CIAR)—for working toward such Dual Agenda change. Chapters Four and Five spell out the details, showing how we frame inquiry, analysis, and action to keep both sides of the Dual Agenda in focus and how the change process has unfolded in different organizations. In Chapter Six, we examine the challenges in this work from the perspective of the CIAR team.

Collaborative Interactive Action Research (CIAR)

CHAPTER 4

Pursuing the Dual Agenda with CIAR

We have made the case for the equity imperative, suggesting that the time has come for work organizations to address issues of gender equity and work–personal life integration, both for their own continued effectiveness and health and for the health of the society of which they are a part. A critical question is *how?* We have argued that the necessary changes cannot be made only at the policy level but must focus on work practices and on the gendered organizational cultures that support them. And we have asserted that each organization needs to design these changes for itself, finding the points of highest leverage — points at which issues of equity and effectiveness intersect — in its own unique culture and way of working. In this and the next two chapters, we present the method we and others are developing to work with organizations on this important task.

Collaborative Interactive Action Research (CIAR) is the name we give to our method. It is designed to uncover gendered assumptions, such as those about competence and commitment, that underlie work practices that are both inequitable and ineffective. Once surfaced, these assumptions can be held up to scrutiny and action plans can be put into place. CIAR creates a context in which individuals and work groups can try to make changes in the way they work.

The underlying premises of this approach—its focus on joint inquiry and collaboration and its commitment to change as well as to the study of organizational systems—are neither new nor unique. CIAR stands squarely within the action research tradition, which started with Lewin's famous belief that you cannot understand an organization without trying to change it, and has developed in many directions since.[1] It is similar also to certain approaches to consultation and cultural analysis.[2] What is different about our approach is that the changes we seek must meet the Dual Agenda, linking organizational goals (equity and effectiveness) that are usually assumed to be adversarial. So while in theory the method is not so different from other forms of action research, in practice it presents unique challenges because its objective is so counterintuitive.

Creating Systemic Change with CIAR

To state the obvious, Dual Agenda change happens only when individuals—either alone or in concert—take action to make it happen. The manager we mentioned in Chapter Three who decided not to give kudos to people who pulled all-nighters was acting as an individual. Such brave individual actions can, in some cases, have a big local impact. But if changes are to take root in an organization, they must be based on more than one person's actions, important as those may be. Lasting impact will not occur without a common language and a shared understanding of the issues involved. Systemic change requires a collective opportunity to reflect on work practices, to discuss and discern the intended and unintended consequences of the status quo, and to develop a shared desire to change. To achieve the results we seek, something must occur to change the way issues of equity and effectiveness are commonly understood; there has to be an occasion for a new, collective understanding to emerge.

CIAR provides for this occasion of shared learning and reframing of organizational experience. Each of its elements— research, action, and interactive collaboration—is critical. *Interactive collaboration* means embarking on a journey of exploration in which external researchers bring expertise about the potential benefits of Dual Agenda change to internal constituents who have equally important expertise about the inner workings of the system and what it will take to change things for the better. This type of collaboration is based on the principle that the difficult work of identifying and questioning deeply held assumptions requires a relational context, in which interactions are characterized by mutuality and fluid expertise—with the expert role shifting back and forth between the CIAR team and the organization. Though the research team brings considerable skill and experience, we do not advise in the traditional consulting sense of providing prescriptions to solve the problems the organization has identified. Rather, we see ourselves as co-learners in a process of mutual inquiry, resisting gendered expectations of what it means to be "an expert" and modeling instead a mode of working that relies on the wisdom of the collective over dependence on the contributions of a few highly skilled individuals.

Whereas most action research projects emphasize collaboration and joint exploration and most face the dilemma of how to demonstrate a type of competence that is not prescriptive and does not offer a definitive set of recommendations, these characteristics have a special significance in a CIAR project. Beliefs and assumptions about organizational change, like all systems of knowledge about the workplace, are subject to the same gendered assumptions about the separation of spheres—and what type of behavior is appropriate for each sphere—that we described in Chapter Two. What is special, therefore, about our approach is that we see the collaboration and joint exploration not only as *different* from typical interactions with organizations but also as *gendered*. That is, norms of collaboration, joint inquiry, and mutuality are more closely aligned with the domestic sphere of life and thus with the "feminine" than they are with the public domain of paid work. This means that reactions and questions about our *method* (and our competence) are going to engage some of the same deeply held beliefs about gender identity and gender expectations that make the *content* of the change work difficult. These effects of the gender dynamic inherent in our method present some unique challenges and opportunities, especially for teams that are all female. We describe these challenges and learnings as we describe how we put CIAR into practice.

The *research* part of CIAR refers to the process of surfacing underlying assumptions, identifying their role in the way the system works, and showing the links to work practices that may have unintended negative consequences for equity and effectiveness. This creates an opportunity for organizational learning and typically results in new knowledge. Such collective learning is a critical part of the capacity for change. Again, while most action research has the implicit goal of learning, the content of a CIAR project requires that this learning go beyond the organization itself and consider how gendered beliefs about the separation of spheres, a societal rather than an organizational phenomenon, affect common work practices and norms.

The *action* element in CIAR reflects the commitment not only to learn but also to take action to make things better. The goal is to make a visible, measurable change that challenges the identified assumptions in a way that achieves both effectiveness and equity outcomes. However, it is not just the measurable result of the change, but also the *experience* of putting Dual Agenda thinking into action, that is valuable. Trying out the new work practices—seeing their intended and unintended consequences, and experiencing what these changes feel like—brings better understanding of underlying assumptions and the effects they have. Keeping each of these elements of CIAR alive in each stage of the change process is one essential part of the method.

Initiating a Change Effort

People often ask us if we go into an organization talking explicitly about the theories of gendered assumptions and separate spheres that underlie Dual Agenda change. We do not. We begin with the notion of the Dual Agenda itself, establishing the link between equity and effectiveness. Once the concept is introduced, the goal is to create a context of joint learning and discovery about the implications of the link for a particular workplace.

Establishing the Dual Agenda

Introducing Dual Agenda concepts and the particular process of mutual inquiry we use can start with something informational — a talk, a brown-bag lunch, or a series of group discussions. In some instances, CIAR researchers send out readings about Dual Agenda change before their first site visit and then hold information and discussion sessions in small groups.[3] Alternatively, the process can begin with a presentation by one of the researchers, followed by small discussion groups to talk about the implications of the framework presented. Whatever tactic we use must include an opportunity for discussion and learning. As an organizational development professional on a CIAR team commented, starting with some intellectual content and a framework from outside the organization is a powerfully different way of starting a change project. "So often," she states, "we charge ahead with change projects without any time to learn or reflect or to understand how what is happening here is rooted in something much larger than just our local workplace culture."[4]

Though many people are intrigued with the concept of the Dual Agenda, linking gender equity and workplace performance is counterintuitive to most models of organizational success. So while initially there is likely to be some excitement and energy, moving from the concept to its implications for this workplace is not straightforward. One way to make the concept more concrete is to start with the presenting problem and connect it to the other side of the Dual Agenda. Let us explain.

The opportunity for change most often arises from either an equity or an effectiveness problem (see Exhibit 4.1.). If the problem is related to gender equity or work–personal life conflict,

Exhibit 4.1. Some Presenting Problems Susceptible to a Dual Agenda Approach.

Problems Related to Gender Equity or Work–Personal Life Integration

- Difficulties in recruiting and retaining women
- Lack of women in leadership positions
- Symptoms of employee stress and burnout, such as high rates of illness and absenteeism

Problems Related to Workplace Performance

- Excessive overtime
- Absenteeism
- Operating in continual crisis mode
- Difficulty meeting deadlines
- Difficulty achieving goals of employee empowerment, working collaboratively, flexibility, speed

the CIAR researchers need to put effectiveness issues on the table so that the initiative is seen as strategic and work practices are fair game for intervention. Conversely, if the presenting problem is more work-related, it is important to link to equity in the early stages to establish a basis for challenging gendered assumptions when they surface.

When the presenting problem is effectiveness, it is tempting to downplay the link to equity early on in the hope that it will make things easier if we just stay with "business" issues and let the equity issues emerge. We have learned the hard way that not making this equity link clear at the start severely limits the chances for Dual Agenda success in the long run. In one organization, for example, an internal change agent invited a

CIAR team to conduct an organizational evaluation, a kind of cultural audit, which the CEO had requested to assess the impact of goals he had set forth to change the way the organization did its work. Two of those goals—to reduce unmanageable workloads without letting go of high standards and to create a "worker-friendly" environment for a diverse staff—related directly to Dual Agenda issues. But even though the researchers and the internal change agent who contacted them were clear about the Dual Agenda implications of these issues, the project went forward without making the connection explicit. We were afraid that to push too much on the equity side would jeopardize the project, eliminating the chance of dealing with the issues. We decided to forge ahead, believing that when we focused on the work issues, gender equity and work–personal life implications would emerge. And indeed they did. The feedback of those findings to a leadership group generated a lot of energy for change, but the energy dissipated quickly and the project died not long after. There was no context for taking up the challenge the Dual Agenda analysis posed to the established culture, which defined workload problems strictly in terms of performance and diversity only in terms of multiculturalism and not in work–personal life arrangements.

When the presenting problem is equity, it is easier to make the link to the other half of the Dual Agenda, at least initially. Many people consider it good news to hear that improving equity can have a positive effect on performance issues. Nonetheless, we have learned that while there may be initial interest in the link, putting it into practice still presents many challenges. When work–personal life issues are the presenting problem, the sponsors of the change initiative often have preconceived notions of what specific changes they would like to see implemented. In many sites, for example, we find that the stress of trying to "balance" has led people to imagine solutions that would make balancing easier, like flextime or work-at-home options. Though these might in fact be appropriate for a Dual Agenda change project, their form and substance are likely to change significantly when effectiveness issues are brought into the picture. Rigid or formulaic flextime programs simply substitute one arbitrary timing (say, 7:00 to 3:00) for another (9:00 to 5:00). A Dual Agenda approach to this issue would look creatively at the *work*, keeping time and place as leverage points for change. However, because the demands and requirements of the work are usually givens in work–personal life initiatives, it can be difficult for people to engage with this way of thinking about flexibility. Because it is so hard to believe that embedded work practices can or will change and because effectiveness and performance have so often been used in the past as reasons to *deny* flexibility, there may be a lot of resistance to talking about the effectiveness issue. Nonetheless, it is important for the CIAR team to call attention to these issues and engage a discussion about what is different about a Dual Agenda change and what this kind of change might look like in this particular organization. Without such a preliminary vision, it is difficult to keep the two halves of the Dual Agenda on the table as the process moves to implementation.

Although it is important to make the Dual Agenda link early on, we want to reiterate that because of the deeply embedded nature of the assumption that equity and effectiveness are adversarial, this connection cannot be sustained uninterrupted no matter how clear or explicit it is. The challenge of holding on to both parts of the Dual Agenda will continually surface and resurface, especially in the implementation phase of work practice change. And as described in Chapter Three, in some cases the equity goals will get lost and in some cases the performance and focus on the needs of the work will disappear. It is connecting these two issues repeatedly that occasions opportunities for joint learning—for our partners in the workplace as well as for us as CIAR researchers.[5]

Engaging Top Management

Successful Dual Agenda change requires the engagement of top management as part of the process. The optimal situation is to have been invited in by top management. Such an entry creates the greatest likelihood that the project will connect to strategic concerns and opens the possibility that the work group at the top will address its own Dual Agenda issues. In the long run, both of these conditions are necessary for lasting change.

Engaging Top Management from the Top.   The advantages of coming in with top management support are illustrated by the case of an executive who launched an initiative on work–personal life integration shortly after becoming controller of a large service provider. This organization was a major regional player in a core service industry, facing serious competition for the first time in its ninety-year history. The new controller had been recruited from a major manufacturing firm that had entered the era of global competition in the early 1980s, with a brief to help make the company competitive in its changed industry environment. Immediately on arrival, he set some high goals for performance improvement in the hundred-person organization. For example, he accelerated the deadlines for external financial reporting following the close of each period, he committed the organization to provide regular briefings for senior management on current accounting issues, and he defined a new role for the controller's group that looked beyond financial reporting to providing support for strategic decision making. At the same time, because he had been involved in a Dual Agenda project at his previous firm, he began to raise the issue of work–personal life integration with the directors who made up his management team.[6]

To the controller, as well as the directors, most of the organization appeared *not* to have serious work–personal life conflicts, mainly because the office generally emptied out by 5:00 or 5:30. Yet he was struggling with his own overwork problem, finding it difficult to carve out sufficient time or keep regular hours with his family and lacking time for exercise or "white space" to read and reflect, either at work or at home. He also observed a number of the directors under severe stress, and he worried about them. So he persisted in creating a team to consider work–personal life issues, even though he lacked strong support for it in the directors' group and encountered skepticism when he talked about it with other corporate executives. When the team proposed a Dual Agenda project, he was open to the idea of looking at business issues and work–personal life issues together.

The controller's acceptance of the Dual Agenda concept had a major impact at various key points in the change initiative. Following an initial survey conducted as a needs assessment, he convened the entire organization to hear and discuss the survey results, which showed that a significant percentage of both male and female staff were struggling with work–personal life conflicts. With the controller and directors listening and taking the issue seriously, it became legitimate for the organization as a whole.

Subsequently, as the project went forward, he put work–personal life conflict on the table in the team-building work of the directors' group, creating a safe space for people to speak openly and surface dysfunctional norms associated with overwork. "It was like an Alcoholics Anonymous meeting," said one director. "Suddenly it was OK to talk about the problems I was having." Many of the top management group also participated in the interviewing phase of the Dual Agenda work. An hour-long interview with the controller uncovered his perception of both organizational constraints on work–personal life integration and his own work–personal life issues.

For this individual, the unpredictability of the need to be present in the office was a problem. "At the senior level, it's almost like they own you," he commented. One way he managed that was through a self-designed policy of "reciprocity." That is, he made up for some of the nights he stayed late by taking off a bit early on days when he was not in demand. He also sometimes worked from home, in particular to handle the heavy volume of e-mail correspondence he received. As the interview progressed, the controller and the action researcher explored how his individual adaptations might actually contribute to the culture of overwork because they were not visible to the rest of his organization. He noted, for example, that when he sent e-mails from home at midnight, people might assume he was working all the time, when in reality he might have spent the afternoon and evening with his family and simply logged on for a while late at night, after the kids were in bed. In fact, a couple of the directors did mention receiving those midnight e-mails.

The fact that the leader and top management group were willing to examine their own practices and assumptions made it much more likely that change would be possible. That willingness was particularly tested in a feedback session—again, an assembly of the entire organization—at which the action researchers described some of the underlying assumptions they had uncovered. One of those assumptions, that "change is free," spoke directly to the impact of the controller's own efforts to reshape the organization to meet the demands of a more competitive environment. Within a year of joining the company, he had launched new strategic objectives, more rigorous performance standards, new accounting software, and several organizational development initiatives, including the Dual Agenda project itself; and all of this came on top of a major restructuring and downsizing that had taken place a couple of years before.

As desirable and essential as the changes were, looking at work practices from a Dual Agenda perspective revealed the unanticipated costs of having so many initiatives going on at once. Understandably, this situation exacerbated work–personal life conflicts for many people in the organization. But it also undermined the controller's own goals, by limiting, for example, the time and resources available for critical change activities like learning new tools, developing new ways of working together, and integrating new people. The quality of work was suffering as people spread their time across competing change efforts, while the energy of the organization was sapped by feelings that the only reward for making positive changes was more change work.

This feedback was difficult for management to hear, and there was considerable tension in the organizationwide meeting at which it was presented. Yet the controller's commitment to the Dual Agenda concept and his participation in the project along the way enabled him and the organization to move through this critical juncture. Later one work group devised a pilot experiment to address the "change is free" assumption, among others, by taking greater control over setting its priorities and organizing its work in ways that would enable it to be more proactive in responding to the need for change while giving individual group members greater flexibility in managing their workloads.

Engaging Top Management from Below.   Having this kind of top management support at the outset is ideal, but it is rare. More often the call for change originates lower in the hierarchy. But even without initiation at the top, there still are effective ways to begin the process and keep connected to top management.

First, it makes sense to include top managers in informational events like brown-bag lunches or presentations, perhaps even by volunteering to give them a preview of whatever intellectual content will be covered in larger sessions. Second, it is particularly helpful to interview top management with the same format as others, focusing on each manager's personal story and experience of these issues rather than on his or her role as positional leader. Finally, it is useful to negotiate some way of giving periodic updates to managers. An example is a CIAR team that established up-front that whenever team members were on site, they would end their visit with a brief meeting with some members of top management to give them an update and debrief on what the team was learning about the organization.

It is important in all these interactions to make sure that they occasion joint learning, in which the researchers offer something of value (their outside perspective on an organization the managers care about) and at the same time listen carefully to the managers' responses to these insights, adopting a stance of inquiry rather than advocacy. We have learned that if managers' concerns—for example, concerns about the quality of the work or concerns about how the proposed change is going to affect their own life and workload—are silenced or not taken fully into account, the project cannot succeed in the long term.

Data Collection

The heart of the data collection step is interactive collaboration—the process of mutual inquiry through which it becomes possible to identify underlying assumptions. CIAR researchers may use a variety of tools to gather data: surveys, field observations of work, interviews, roundtables. From the research perspective, a range of sources is desirable in order to bring a credible degree of independent judgment to the change effort. But this cannot be a process in which outsiders gather data, take it away, and later return with a diagnosis and "solution" of the organization's problems. Rather, the final analysis develops from an evolutionary process of shared discovery and sense making. Each action by the researchers—asking questions, raising issues, making observations, listening to people's responses—constitutes an intervention and represents a key step along the way. Conducting research in this way is essential for achieving a Dual Agenda outcome that people in the organization will embrace and sustain, precisely because the whole Dual Agenda concept is so contradictory to the way people usually think about work.

Starting with a Survey

Sometimes, as in the case of the controller's organization, it is necessary to start the data collection step in the spirit of "needs assessment." Then a survey can be an effective way to document and confirm that there are gender equity or work–personal life issues and can help generate agreement about the validity of the Dual Agenda approach. In the controller's case, the survey instrument, which was designed jointly by the company's human resource department and a CIAR team, asked respondents one broadly framed question: "In general, how satisfied are you with the balance between your work and personal life?" In addition, it asked them to indicate on a scale of 1 to 5 their level of agreement with a series of twelve statements about work and work–personal life conflicts (see Exhibit 4.2).

Another section of the survey asked respondents to indicate the number of days they had missed work for various possible reasons—a list of ten, including personal illness, the illness of a child, lack of child care, and lack of elder care. Finally, it asked for basic demographic information, such as age, sex, and marital status; and it invited respondents to state any concerns about work–personal life conflicts not raised in the survey questions.

Virtually everyone in this organization completed the survey, and most employees attended the kickoff meeting at which the results were presented. The survey indicated that overall,

Exhibit 4.2. Work–Personal Life Survey.

Please indicate the extent to which you agree with each of the following statements. Use the following rating scale: *1 = strongly disagree; 2 = disagree; 3 = agree somewhat; disagree somewhat; 4 = agree; 5 = strongly agree; NA = not applicable.*

_____ In order for me to achieve work–personal life balance, some of my work does not get done.

_____ I am unable to communicate effectively at work because of time constraints.

_____ The amount of work I have to do is about right.

_____ The number of hours I work each day is about right.

_____ I feel it is often necessary to work through lunch to get work done.

_____ I have been unable to schedule vacation due to work pressures.

_____ I use vacation days because I am reluctant to use other company-sponsored time off due to a culture that discourages or penalizes absences.

_____ My personal and family responsibilities interfere with my ability to meet my work responsibilities.

_____ My work responsibilities interfere with my ability to meet my personal and family responsibilities.

_____ In order to handle my work and family responsibilities, I spend less time on my own needs.

_____ The amount of stress I experience on the job causes my work performance to suffer.

_____ The amount of stress I experience due to family or personal pressures causes my work performance to suffer.

Source: Questions based on a survey prepared by Mary Young.

managers and staff in the controller's organization were about evenly divided on satisfaction with work–personal life balance: 31 percent dissatisfied or very dissatisfied; 35 percent satisfied or very satisfied; and 35 percent neither satisfied nor dissatisfied. However, broken down by sex, the data showed that the men had put themselves in the satisfied columns by a margin of 2 to 1, while the pattern for the women was just the reverse—40 percent of the women indicated *dissatisfaction*; only 24 percent said they were satisfied with the balance between work and personal life. Answers to the more specific questions also revealed that women were more likely than men to have personal-life issues interfere with work—or at least to be more comfortable in acknowledging interference. Yet a majority of both sexes—53 percent of the men and 72 percent of the women—indicated that they often worked through lunch to get their work done and, by the same percentages, that they sacrificed personal needs in order to meet their obligations to both work and family. In the face of these data, it was impossible to deny that work–personal life integration was an important issue, and the survey opened up the space for people to discuss it.

During the feedback session, the CIAR team divided the organization into its actual work groups and asked each group to examine its work practices through the lens of work–personal life integration—that is, to consider what aspects of "the way things are done around here" contributed to whatever conflicts group members experienced in trying to function effectively in both spheres. Next, the researchers asked the groups to come up with ideas for changes that would be good for *both* work and work–personal life integration and to report back to the whole organization at the end. The result was striking. In a very short period, the work groups collectively came up with dozens of ideas for Dual Agenda changes, which raised a fundamental question: If ideas for change were so readily available, why had changes not been made? In combination with the survey results, this simple "thought experiment" became a significant intervention that set the controller's organization up to look for underlying assumptions that supported established patterns and made change difficult.

The usefulness of the data gathered in initial surveys is limited, but the exercise in and of itself can make an important contribution to a change initiative. These surveys tend to have high response rates. People put energy into the exercise because they care about the issues, and in some cases they are suffering with issues that are typically silenced. One other reason to do a survey is that some people can "hear" data better in quantitative as opposed to qualitative form, so it is a way to reach more people. A survey provides a chance to make an intervention on a broad basis in a large organization, but it need not be used exclusively for large groups. Surveys can be useful in groups as small as twenty.

Individual Interviews

With or without the setup provided by an initial survey, the CIAR team begins to make the systemic link between work practice and work-life integration in individual interviews. These interviews are loosely structured around open-ended topics. They approach work–personal life issues through individual stories, focusing, for example, on what goes on in a typical day and how long it is or on what the person would change in the company's work norms to make it easier to integrate work and personal life. To get to issues of equity, an interviewer might pose questions such as "What do you see as the most important contribution you make here? Is it recognized and rewarded?" "What advice would you give someone to succeed here? Would you give different advice to men and to women? To a person of color?"

Fluid expertise becomes important as the participants in the interview work together to examine the organization through the lens of either gender equity or work–personal life integration. The interviewer is in inquiry mode in these conversations—gathering information and exploring why people think or feel the way they do, not trying to change their minds. Another essential aspect of the CIAR method in individual interviews is to begin the process of reframing issues from the individual to the systemic level. For example, following up on the question about length of the workday, the interviewer might probe why a person is choosing to work certain hours. What is the workload? What are expectations about being present in the office? What are the demands of meetings or travel? All of these shift the attention from an individual's problem to system expectations that account for this problem.

To reframe issues of competence, the interviewer might raise the question of performance evaluations and the signals about competence they convey. Or the reframing might be accomplished by providing an outsider's perspective and language, for example, by observing that late meetings exclude the voices and expertise of a certain population—those who have family or other outside commitments—and noting that this situation affects quality as well as equity. These are micro-interventions, and they are an important part of the process. They help open up assumptions for discussion and evaluation, in many cases simply by creating the occasion for people to ask themselves why they do the things they do, to entertain doubt, and then possibly to come up with alternative approaches.

Such individual interactions are time-consuming. In the end, however, they actually help the process move faster, largely because in individual, confidential conversations, people tend to feel more comfortable raising topics or expressing views they do not consider appropriate for discussion in the group as a whole. Later the CIAR team can aggregate these issues as part of its feedback to the group in a way that preserves anonymity but opens up topics that may not usually be discussable. In many organizational cultures, this is the only way to bring to light the pain around work–personal life conflicts that people, especially men, tend to feel they must suffer in silence.

Roundtables: Group Discussions and Context-Specific Surveys

As data collection proceeds, the mutual inquiry gains momentum and greater focus through group discussions we have labeled "roundtables." These provide a setting for the researchers to try out ideas that are emerging in the team's analysis and to get a sense of how widespread some of the individual issues might be. They also help legitimate topics that had previously been undiscussable. For example, in one roundtable, composed of some people who had been interviewed and some who had not, the personal costs of the way time was used in the organization began to be talked about. The pattern of "throwing time at problems" became quite clear in that discussion and was a valuable piece of the analysis.

A survey conducted partway through data gathering can take on the characteristics of a roundtable. This is a different kind of survey from the ones conducted at the beginning of a project, in that its items are based on prior interviews and discussions and reflect an informed sense of what work practices to explore. It uses the organization's language, addresses context-specific issues, and reflects an emerging understanding of organizational patterns. The example in Exhibit 4.3 (see pp. 94–96)—part of an extensive survey on work practices, effectiveness, and work–personal life integration developed for a nongovernmental organization (NGO)—provides an illustration.

Like an initial survey, this instrument can confirm that a problem exists, but it can go beyond that to provide data on the links between equity or work–personal life issues and specific work practices. Thus it is a much more significant intervention in the system. This kind of survey can open up the organization to innovative thinking by getting people talking about the roots of work practices. The feedback of the survey results, done in a collaborative, interactive way, becomes an opportunity for a conversation about issues at a deep level.

Data Analysis

The emergence of an analysis begins in the phase of data gathering and proceeds interactively with people in the organization. Yet the formal analysis, when the CIAR team steps back to review and interpret all of the data together, is a critical point in the project. The goal of this step is to hold up a mirror for the organization that enables it to recognize and name underlying assumptions and understand their impact. It is the key contribution of the research part of CIAR and provides an occasion for collective reflection and learning. It is a place that usually requires an outsider's perspective.

Identifying Underlying Assumptions: A Detailed Example

The thought process that goes into the framing of underlying assumptions begins with the CIAR team reviewing all the data while asking itself questions such as "What does an ideal worker look like here?" "What do people do to demonstrate competence here?" and "What kind of behavior gets recognized here?"[7] In the case of the NGO mentioned earlier, answering these questions helped the team see that the definition of competence in that organization was closely linked to the demonstration of intellectual prowess. The researchers used the words of interviewees to elaborate on this point, drawing up a list of possible quotes to use in the feedback session, such as the one from a manager who said, "What's important here are your ideas, not your position." The high value placed on *new* ideas, in particular, reflected the NGO's sense of identity as an innovative organization, providing "smart money" and cutting-edge research to the field of international development. This emphasis meant that intellectual contributions were assumed to be more important than other, less visible ones such as grant administration, monitoring, and assessment in the implementation of the NGO's basic task of making grants. "It's the up-front work [in new projects] that is the most rewarded and most respected," said another staff member. "Once the idea is there, it's no longer such a big deal, or so much fun." The CIAR team named this assumption "Competence Equals New Ideas."

Once we discerned this pattern, we could move the analysis to a higher level of inquiry. Why was this assumption in place? What reality did it describe? What positive contributions was it making, or had it made in the past, to the organization's success? How well did it correspond to the present environment? How well did it support the organization's strategic direction?

In the case of Competence Equals New Ideas, the high value placed on intellectual contributions reflected the success this NGO had achieved in creating a distinctive niche and an international reputation as a donor. The idea of empowerment through knowledge was a central element of its sense of mission and a strong motivator for its staff. The emphasis on new ideas also supported an environment of intellectual curiosity and continuous improvement. This

(continued on p. 96)

Exhibit 4.3. NGO Survey: Sample Questions.

I. Strategic Directions and Organizational Effectiveness

Interviews with staff at NGO identified a number of strategic elements that staff believe are important to NGO's effectiveness and ability to achieve its mission. Please indicate below the extent to which you believe the following elements (a) are important to NGO's effectiveness in achieving the mission and (b) are currently being realized within your work group, team, or unit.

Please use the following rating system: *1 = unimportant; 2 = not very important; 3 = neutral; 4 = important; 5 = very important; NA = not applicable.*

_____ Working closely with grantees in project development

_____ Mobilizing support for new opportunities for development-oriented research

_____ Synthesizing results of projects NGO has funded

_____ Scouting out research talent in developing countries

_____ Mobilizing external funding from other donors

II. Work

This section asks about the way work is accomplished at NGO. Please indicate the extent to which you agree or disagree with the following statements. *1 = strongly disagree; 2 = disagree; 3 = agree somewhat, disagree somewhat; 4 = agree; 5 = strongly agree; NA = not applicable.*

A. Work Practices

_____ I spend a significant amount of my work week lobbying for management support for my projects or preparing status updates to managers and directors.

_____ Without sacrificing the services I provide to internal clients and external recipients and partners, some of my job could be streamlined or eliminated.

B. Work Structuring

_____ Operating procedures within NGO enhance efficient work processes.

C. Reward Systems

_____ Staying at the cutting edge in one's field is rewarded at NGO.

III. Work Groups

This section asks about the way work is accomplished within your work group. Please indicate the extent to which you agree or disagree with the following statements. *1 = strongly disagree; 2 = disagree; 3 = agree somewhat, disagree somewhat; 4 = agree; 5 = strongly agree; NA = not applicable.*

I spend a significant amount of time on the following activities:

_____ Coordinating and planning work with others

_____ Peer review of the work of others

_____ Participating in work group decision making

_____ Responding to requests for input from others

_____ Dealing with crises

_____ Mobilizing complementary funding

_____ Playing the role of manager rather than advising research

IV. Work and Personal Life

To what extent would the following affect your ability to integrate your work and personal life in the way you want? *1 = strongly hinder; 2 = hinder; 3 = have no effect; 4 = help; 5 = strongly help; NA=not applicable.*

_____ Improving my work group's operating efficiency

_____ Changing NGO's culture to be more concerned with output than with time put in

_____ Changing my immediate manager to be more concerned with output than with time put in

_____ Streamlining or eliminating nonessential parts of my job

_____ Calibrating my hours to match the ebb and flow of work

_____ Adding administrative, professional, or technical assistance to my work group

(continued)

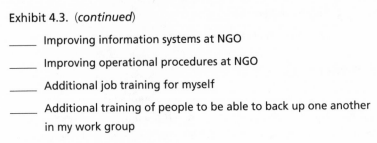

Exhibit 4.3. (*continued*)

_____ Improving information systems at NGO

_____ Improving operational procedures at NGO

_____ Additional job training for myself

_____ Additional training of people to be able to back up one another in my work group

Source: Partially adapted from a survey prepared by Mary Young.

helped make the NGO a challenging, exciting place to work and enabled it to attract highly talented and committed people.

With these positive contributions in mind, we shifted the analysis to the Dual Agenda. What were the consequences of this assumption for gender equity and work–personal life integration? For organizational effectiveness? The CIAR team found a number of unintended negative consequences attached to the Competence Equals New Ideas assumption. In terms of effectiveness, this meant that people were being unwittingly discouraged from doing the essential work of monitoring and assessing the impact of current projects, tasks that were becoming increasingly important from a strategic point of view. In particular, the premium the organization placed on generating new projects worked against an emerging need for the NGO to adapt to a changed environment, in which increased competition for resources made it necessary to devote greater energy to fundraising and to be more strategically focused on grant making with more limited resources. In this culture, fundraising tended to be grouped with the less exciting and less intellectually challenging tasks, and this worked against the organization's effort to make it a higher priority. At the same time, the constant push for new ideas and the proliferation of new projects created little incentive, and left little time, for grant makers to reflect on and evaluate ongoing projects. Because new ideas were the most valued currency in the NGO's culture, they were difficult to resist, even when saying no to a new project might enhance the quality of current work or be better strategically for the organization.

There were also unintended consequences for gender equity from this definition of competence. The workload implications of the pressures on grant-making staff to keep producing new ideas and launching new projects, including the heavy travel requirements entailed in that kind of work, made this NGO an unfriendly environment for people with significant outside commitments, at least in the ranks of the highest-status staff, the grant makers. Women were disproportionately underrepresented in those ranks. At the same time, they were significantly overrepresented in the lower-status staff positions responsible for grant administration and monitoring, where they bore the brunt of the organization's tendency to devalue competence in areas assumed to be less skill-intensive and less cutting-edge. Thus even though the NGO was committed to advancing equity in the world, its seemingly gender-neutral definition of competence was contributing to an inequitable situation inside its own organization.

In the final step of the analysis, we identified leverage points for action that could enhance both equity and effectiveness without undermining the positive contributions the assumptions might be making. In the case of Competence Equals New Ideas, the CIAR team suggested that the organization might consider specific ways to develop a more critical approach to evaluating new ideas and new projects, an approach that could make saying no to starting something new a legitimate option for a variety of reasons, including being more selective, giving other tasks a higher priority, and maintaining a manageable workload. Another suggestion was to look for ways to recognize a wider range of contributions so that generating new ideas would not be the only way to demonstrate competence.

Just how much impact an analysis can have, in and of itself, remains an open question in Dual Agenda work. Yet in each project, the CIAR team's presentation of its findings is a defining moment. It provides an occasion for collective reflection and begins the process of creating a common language to use

in discussing and deepening understanding of the issues involved. The analysis is crucial for framing and setting up a formal
intervention—an experimental change in work practices—but
it is also an intervention in its own right. As Maureen Harvey
points out, "We intervene with ideas, new vocabulary, an analysis, an outsider point of view, long-term focus, and a mission."[8]
All of this comes together in the feedback step.

Feedback

Feedback is an iterative process. Although it is tempting to think
of feedback as occurring only in a formal setting, in fact feedback often begins early in the process of data collection. A CIAR
team works on-site for a number of days conducting interviews
and discussing internally the themes that seem to be emerging.
Before leaving, the researchers share these preliminary findings
with key groups in the organization, for example, the contact
group and the management team. Sharing the analysis at this
formative stage enables the researchers to conduct a "reality
check" on their understanding of the issues and to expand and
deepen their analysis with the benefit of the perspective of organizational insiders. At the same time, this early feedback is
another micro-intervention. It provides a look at organizational
issues through a gender lens or a lens of work–personal life integration and an opportunity for members of the organization
to reflect on the meanings that such a lens uncovers.[9]

Preparing the Formal Feedback

Once the CIAR team has developed a full-blown analysis and
is preparing for a more formal feedback presentation, it is valuable to present the findings in a preliminary way to the management group. The goal is to create a context in which group

members can fully engage the ideas and can consider the possible implications for their own behavior, as managers and even in their personal lives. This is an important step in continuing to engage top management. It can prevent the members of the group from feeling blindsided by the analysis, and in the best case it can enable them to play an active role in the feedback. In one preliminary session, for example, the managers suggested changes about how to present the analysis to make it more effective, including avoiding some phrases that in the vernacular of that organization could give miscues about the team's meaning. In another instance, they helped connect Dual Agenda issues to the strategic concerns of the business.

In one corporate setting, an early feedback session with three top managers became a very intense working session in which the executives brought in their own examples, understood the analysis at a deep level, and began to embrace it. During this session, other members of the organization circled the meeting room nervously. They expected censorship and could hardly believe the actual result—the managers proposed only one insignificant word change. A key factor in this outcome was that the managers' having a chance to question the team about the implications of the findings and to experience the team's stance of inquiry and empathy helped them personalize the Dual Agenda. Connecting it to broader issues in society seemed to have an especially positive effect, as one manager noted, "What you are really saying is that it's not that we do things wrong here, it's just that we are reflecting larger patterns in society. But we can decide to do something about it." Subsequently, in the larger feedback session, these managers took on the role of explaining parts of the analysis. This was a particularly nice illustration of CIAR as an iterative, cumulative change process.[10]

Giving the Feedback

When the moment for formal presentation of the Dual Agenda analysis arrives, it is important that the structure of the meeting and the mode of feedback be designed to include time for both discussion and a plan for moving to action. For the analysis to have the desired impact, the audience for the feedback presentation needs to be as inclusive as possible, inviting entire departments, work groups, or units and making sure that everyone—from secretaries and technicians to managers and supervisors—is invited. The analysis is about the work culture, and everyone in the group experiences its effects, even if not all have been interviewed.

A useful framework is to give the analysis in four parts: This is what we heard. This is what we think it means. This is what we think the consequences are. These are potential leverage points for change. It is important to avoid an overly academic or didactic style of presentation. This can be accomplished, for example, by using the language of the organization even though in some cases the team might feel it does not capture the nuances of the analysis as well as some more abstract terms might. In addition, the researchers must continuously link to the organization's mental frame or risk having the organization reject out of hand an analysis that is likely to seem counterintuitive. It can be very productive in a feedback session to present the analysis and then break out into small working groups to discuss ideas for action. But this will work only if the feedback is given in such a way that the groups connect with the analysis and feel open to using it, adapting it, and making it their own.

The cases in which the Dual Agenda analysis has been the most powerful have been those in which everyone in the organization, particularly all levels of the hierarchy, heard the feedback together. In these instances, the researchers can set a tone of inquiry during discussion of the findings, which helps people in the organization begin to trust the work and to accept that the CIAR team is not just imposing its own viewpoint or acting as a mouthpiece of either management or the group that invited it in.

These sessions become powerful when they provide an occasion and a safe place for dealing with the "undiscussables"— the issues that normally operate below the surface of what is considered appropriate conversation. A dramatic example of this phenomenon occurred in the presentation of an analysis that described an underlying assumption that "time is cheap." When a senior manager suggested that "time is no obstacle" would be a more accurate statement of this assumption, one brave junior staff member objected. She noted that in the ranks, it *felt* like management's view was indeed that employees' time was a commodity to be expended with little consideration of the cost. Her challenge both opened up the conversation and forced consideration of concrete changes in work practices aimed at placing a higher value on people's time.

By contrast, in an instance in which the CIAR team gave its feedback to the leadership group only, there was a lively discussion of issues that included identifying ideas for change. But this discussion was limited to topics important to professional and management personnel, glossing over serious issues raised by the administrative support staff, who had no voice in the conversation. This meeting seemed very productive in the moment but in the long run created more disillusionment than momentum for change. In another case, the feedback meeting was limited to the group that had volunteered to do a pilot experiment with work practice changes. Because of this limitation, the group found it difficult to get the support it needed, both to carry out the experiment and, subsequently, to diffuse its learning to the larger organization.

The feedback presentation is the moment in a CIAR project when the Dual Agenda concept generates the most excitement and support. Although its success depends on the extensive prior work that has been done—the interviews and micro-interventions with individuals—the feedback session itself is important because it provides a rare occasion for collective reflection and learning. Because it gives everyone a common language and creates a common "narrative" about equity and effectiveness, it is an intervention in its own right and can lead to small but important individually initiated local changes. As Deborah Kolb and Deborah Merrill-Sands write, "What we have learned [in this project] is that when one brings deep cultural assumptions to the surface and promotes narratives around them, one enhances people's capacities to take actions in their organizations that promote the dual aims of equity and effectiveness."[11]

Moving to Action

Feedback of the analysis, by providing an alternative interpretation of how the existing system works, has the power to open the organization to innovation. Some individuals, on their own, will make changes in the way they work, talk about issues, or interact with others. As important as these individual changes are, we believe it is even more important to create an opportunity for some sort of collective change effort, an effort that will require continued discussion, modification, and evaluation of Dual Agenda implications. The real challenge is to tap into individuals' increased capacity and openness and translate that into collective action plans for change that are concrete and doable and that can be experienced and evaluated on both dimensions of the Dual Agenda.

One way to start this collective process is to incorporate small group work into the feedback design. For example, the presentation and large group discussion can be followed by "buzz groups" to talk about what aspects of the analysis were most engaging. This gives people time to work with the analysis and apply it, in concrete terms, to their own work groups before they move to creating action plans. In one organization, the CIAR team ended its feedback presentation by assigning people to groups based on their work affiliations and giving them discussion questions that focused on which of the assumptions had most relevance for their work and what additional "unintended consequences" they had experienced. After these initial group discussions, people had a chance to join an action-focused group whose task was to determine leverage points and generate action plans.[12]

In moving to action, the CIAR team often starts the discussion with one of the leverage points identified in the analysis. For example, in the Competence Equals New Ideas analysis mentioned earlier, the researchers suggested looking for ways to recognize a wider range of contributions as a leverage point so that generating new ideas would not be the only way to demonstrate competence. One group started with this leverage point and considered possible action plans. The one they decided to develop was a plan to reformulate the composition of their teams so that grants administration, fundraising, and project monitoring and assessment had more weight. But in their discussion, they also developed other leverage points for change and came up with a number of other potential action projects that could be implemented in the future.

One of the most important parts in the work of planning for action is to identify the measures of success. Engaging a discussion about the desired outcomes—for both equity and effectiveness—is an important way to reinforce the importance of addressing both sides of the Dual Agenda in any intervention. We have found this to be one of the liveliest and most interesting parts of the discussion. Groups often come up with creative measures, such as the "reduction of sleepless nights." Exhibit 4.4 shows how one work group envisioned a change it called "work-focused flextime" and how the group planned to assess its impact.

The time and structure needed for this process can vary. In one company, the entire staff took two successive days for brainstorming ideas for work practice changes, alternating between small groups and plenary sessions. The key point is for people not to disperse from the feedback session without making plans for immediate follow-up. This is a critical moment for influencing whether or how the Dual Agenda initiative will move into collective action. In the best case, the entire group is brought back together to hear the action steps that each small group has discussed. This large group works best when everyone has a chance to see the different work practice changes suggested, complete with the list of expected outcomes for equity and effectiveness, and has a chance to discuss them and choose the ones they believe will have the greatest impact. Alternatively, a committee can be set up to review and evaluate proposals and design a process for implementation.

Exhibit 4.4. Work-Focused Flextime: Changes, Desired Results, and Measures of Success.

Changes in Time

- Core hours: 9:30–2:30
- Standard lunch of 45 minutes
- Coverage: 7:00–4:15
- Monthly schedules: standard individual start time per month

Changes in Work

- Schedule meetings during core hours.
- Use "10 Questions" requirements sheet.
- Shift human resources in response to critical times analysis.

Changes in Time: Desired Results

- Increased flexibility
- Reduced commuting time
- Reduced work–personal life stress
- Increased ability to pursue life goals while being productive at work
- Increased employee empowerment

Changes in Work: Desired Results

- Increased productivity in non-core hours (fewer meetings)
- Increased ability to manage work
- Increased number of on-time projects
- Reduced redos with clarity on requirements
- Reduced overtime through shifting of resources at critical times

**Evaluating Success:
Work–Personal Life Measures**

- Hours spent commuting
- Degree of unpredictability in amount of time spent at work
- Degree of satisfaction in integrating work and personal life
- Amount of time spent with family, friends, community

**Evaluating Success:
Work Measures**

- Number of overtime hours
- Number of redos
- Number of on-time projects
- Customer survey on quality, responsiveness, and timeliness

Conclusion

In this chapter, we have emphasized the collaborative, inter-active, and research aspects of CIAR. We have shown how they are intertwined and how they depend on openness and inquiry at all stages of the process. But our main point is that a change effort based on the Dual Agenda creates particular, unique challenges that must be addressed continuously—at initiation of a project, during data collection and data analysis, and when giving feedback. At every step, it is essential to bring equity and effectiveness together. Each such connection is already an intervention; together they prepare the way for a collective change project—the subject of Chapter Five.

CHAPTER 5

Making Change

The process, described in Chapter Four, of identifying underlying assumptions and creating opportunities for discussing their impacts on people's lives and work typically unleashes energy for change and stimulates many creative ideas for what forms the change could take. The action step in Collaborative Interactive Action Research (CIAR) gives people a chance to experience different ways of doing things, shaped by new understanding. This step is often exhilarating, even though the change work is difficult.

Dual Agenda change (aimed at increasing both gender equity and organizational effectiveness) involves getting a feel for what challenging deeply held assumptions—for example, assumptions about commitment and competence or about the place of paid work in one's sense of identity and self-esteem—really entails. Discussion and cognitive learning cannot substitute for that firsthand experience. The essential role of the action step in the change process is captured by a Chinese proverb: "When I hear, I forget. When I see, I remember. When I do, I understand."

We envision the action step as a "small wins" and "small losses" approach.[1] It builds understanding and support for large-scale change by demonstrating concrete outcomes on a small scale. We learn from each work practice change, successful or not, because it uncovers more about the underlying assumptions and especially about what holds those assumptions in place. In fact, as the process unfolds, new insights may alter the definitions of what constitutes a win or a loss. Staying in the mode of mutual inquiry, fundamental to CIAR, is the key to making this iterative process work. In practice, it means creating room for people to raise and address concerns and objections and keeping both parts of the Dual Agenda active at all times. CIAR's framework of experimentation, as well as its emphasis on mutual inquiry, enables this to occur.

Understanding Resistance in the CIAR Context

The intent of the action experiment in CIAR is to change work practices in ways that address the negative consequences of gendered assumptions in a world where roles are no longer neatly divided by sex. What is important to remember, however, is that those assumptions persist in organizations because in times past they have been part of an effectively functioning system. When a work group considers a change that challenges these operative assumptions, it can expect to run into resistance grounded in the experience of past successes, individual and organizational. Indeed, if there is no resistance, CIAR researchers should begin to question whether they and their organizational partners are on the right track. Resistance plays an important role in the process, but it is necessary to avoid dismissing it as recalcitrance rather than creating the context for dealing with the concerns on which it is based.

This attitude toward resistance is not unique to CIAR. But it is particularly relevant for Dual Agenda work, which challenges the most staunchly defended boundary in organizational life—the one that maintains the separation of public and private spheres. Working with resistance is essential because the goal of the Dual Agenda is not to replace one dominant pattern with another—to make masculine gendered organizations into feminine gendered ones or to create a society where family life is privileged over all else. The goal is to create something new— to find creative solutions for existing problems that integrate these different ways of thinking and doing.[2]

Sources of Resistance

There are many sources of such resistance. First, there are concerns about performance. Won't the ranking of a leading university slip if it changes the way it hires and promotes in an effort to attract and retain senior women? How will the work of a business unit get done if people stop staying late to do it? How can I accomplish my career goals if I devote more time and attention to my personal life? Uncovering these concerns and addressing them is a central part of dealing with gendered assumptions. One needs to honor them, and any suggested changes must somehow deal with them.[3] In all cases, it is essential to hold on to both parts of the Dual Agenda—but that *feels* scary. We have results that show this kind of change is possible, yet in each new organizational context, people need to prove it for themselves.

Beyond such immediate performance concerns, there is also often resistance to Dual Agenda change at a structural level because the masculine gendered assumptions it challenges are so deeply embedded in every aspect of work institutions. Human resource policies embody the full-time worker norm in a variety of ways. For example, the use of head count to manage personnel instead of full-time equivalents makes movement toward flexibility, such as job sharing or flextime, extremely difficult. On a larger scale, the Fair Labor Standards Act, which dictates that any work over eight hours a day constitutes overtime to be paid at time and a half, makes flexibility in work hours—such as the forty-hour week made up of four ten-hour days—difficult for nonexempt employees. Even space issues in offices configured with full-time cubicle dwellers in mind can be seen as obstacles to change and thus create resistance to such possibilities as, for example, creating open or shared spaces.

Embedded norms in computer systems, or other aspects of infrastructure, can be another source of resistance. For example, service technicians in one work group wanted to figure out a way to create schedules so that not everybody had to be on call all the time. The group came up with the idea of creating subteams from all the different specialties that could take turns being on call at prespecified times. But the information system could not incorporate this additional level of distinction because it was built on the assumption that all members of this group were completely interchangeable. Such infrastructural barriers lead to resistance because they imply that certain changes just cannot be made.

In most cases, these sources of resistance emerge only as work groups actually begin to change the work practices in which the barriers are embedded. As with individual concerns, when they surface, people can see how they relate to underlying assumptions and how they help hold existing norms in place, even when those norms no longer play a positive role in the organization. It is at this point that the barriers become potential leverage points for action. That is why, in the CIAR method, we emphasize the need to view change as an iterative process in which resistance plays an essential, constructive role.

How Resistance Emerges: An Example

One change initiative undertaken by the agricultural research institute we described in Chapter Three illustrates the process of uncovering layers of resistance and gaining understanding step by step. Several brainstorming sessions by work groups followed the feedback to the whole organization about the culture of individual heroism. One group decided to consider a change that many people had thought about before—indeed, what the whole organization wanted—which was to reduce the number of trips scientists made into the field. These were long, treacherous, harrowing trips over very bad roads, and people were making them once or twice a week. The unstated assumption governing this behavior was that "serious" scientists were "hands-on" and therefore had to make these trips often.

This work practice seemed an excellent candidate for a Dual Agenda experimental change. People thought there were simple technologies available to perform the field research so that local field staff could do some of the things scientists were doing. The change could promote better training and more opportunity for local field staff, while it gave scientists the time to think, write, and work collaboratively with their colleagues. This change would also challenge the assumption that "real" scientists worked primarily out in the field—a belief that slowed the advancement of women scientists, most of whom were unable to make these field trips as frequently as the men. In short, the change addressed both sides of the Dual Agenda, *and* it had wide support.

As the group moved to implement the action experiment, however, people began to see some implications of the change they had not considered before. In particular, they became concerned about exploiting the local field staff by getting them to do scientists' work at regular pay. This was an issue that touched sensitivities about differences of class and race in the organization, which had surfaced clearly in the Dual Agenda analysis. Working it out took quite a long time, but after many joint discussions with the fieldworkers involved, a creative solution emerged based on the idea of using nonmonetary rewards—such as time and training—to recognize the additional responsibilities the field staff would be taking on.

But once it looked as if this experiment was actually going to happen, the planning took an interesting twist: one male scientist who had been one of its strongest supporters began to pull back. He had become very concerned over the inequitable pay issue, but he had also started to feel uncomfortable about being linked to this change. He was a junior member of the organization, a little afraid of sticking his neck out, and he had begun to see the reasons why he had wanted to do this travel. "My career may be on the line if I am the one who is not seen in the field," he said. "And if I don't go, I won't pick up the unexpected bits of information that can be useful, so my work might suffer." The CIAR team quite naturally felt this resistance as a major setback to the action research effort. But in the long run, it helped the group connect with some of the factors that held the assumptions about "real" scientists in place in this institute and created an opportunity to rethink the design of the experiment to address these legitimate concerns.

This example shows the iterative nature of the process and also demonstrates that what an experiment *feels* like cannot be fully anticipated at the start. It is often only when faced with the reality of change that people begin to recognize their own concerns. If the action researchers are able to view these concerns as legitimate, to be honored and respected rather than suppressed, the experiment can move ahead and the collective learning can proceed.

Engaging Resistance: The Experimental Context and Mutual Inquiry

CIAR researchers create the opportunity to proceed iteratively and to engage resistance fully and creatively by framing a Dual Agenda initiative as strictly limited in scope and duration. This experimental frame is critical because when work groups set out to enact their ideas for making Dual Agenda changes, the weight of established procedures and norms can seem overwhelming. So to indicate that an organization will change, say, its head count criteria *just for an experiment* can have an important effect across the system, opening it up to learning and possibly to larger-scale change. The following case illustrates the value of the experimental context and the way in which engaging resistance in a mutual inquiry mode can support moving from analysis into concrete action steps.

The Value of Experimentation: A Detailed Example

The leader of a software engineering group agreed only reluctantly to participate in a work–personal life change initiative. The group was operating under intense pressure to develop a new product, and everyone in this predominantly male organization was working painfully long hours. This situation seemed a perfect site to try a Dual Agenda experiment, but the group leader was concerned about the impact of taking the time necessary to examine and change work practices. Despite this concern, his manager selected the group for a pilot experiment. Since he was unwilling to say no to his boss, the project began, but he moved forward with great skepticism toward the Dual Agenda concept.[4]

After completing the data collection and analysis steps, a CIAR team provided feedback to the group, addressing three underlying gendered assumptions about its work. First was the belief that the "real work" of software engineering—the work for which one would be recognized as competent and would be promoted—was an individual activity. Employees recognized that they had to do a certain amount of "nonreal" work, such as sharing information, providing status reports, and joint problem solving, but that was not something for which they expected to be rewarded. The time spent on those kinds of activities seemed like wasted time. A second and related assumption was that work output was something tangible—a concrete product. Work such as helping or teaching others, passing along information, maintaining lines of communication, and fostering teamwork, which added value by keeping the project moving forward smoothly, did not meet the organization's definition of output. So it was largely invisible as a form of work. Said one engineer, "It is assumed that if nothing bad happened, nothing bad was *going* to happen, and that's not always the case." The third assumption highlighted by the CIAR team was that the organization valued independence and autonomy above all else. Although work was organized by subsystem teams, the general belief among the engineers was that the way to get ahead was through some individual act of heroism, such as solving a high-visibility problem.

These assumptions contributed to a number of business problems, some of which the group recognized and others not. The overarching problem was a continual crisis mode of operation. There was little incentive in this organization to put much time into the kind of work that helped prevent crises from happening. Indeed, people noted a pattern in which the person who caused a problem was then rewarded for solving it.

In addition, since dealing with crises had become the norm, the group tended to respond to *every* issue as a crisis—crisis mode had become the accepted way of working. Managers spoke of manufacturing a crisis in order to get needed resources. Every request for support across subsystem groups was an "urgent" request because people felt that otherwise they would never get attention, and every schedule was a stretch schedule, with unrealistic deadlines. Since crises, stress, and immediacy were the norm, people had little motivation to establish priorities. If an engineer ran into a problem and needed help or information, it was considered OK to interrupt whomever he or she needed to get the answers immediately. Or if someone got involved in solving a problem, it was OK to miss a meeting or an appointment. In this crisis culture, needing to solve a problem was an acceptable excuse that required no further explanation.

The crisis culture had negative implications for the group's ability to launch its new product on time and on budget, as well as for the engineers' ability to integrate work into a satisfying personal life. There was a strong tendency in this organization to throw time at problems—to work the same way, only harder and longer—rather than to look for different ways of doing the work. This meant that the ability to throw time at problems was a desirable attribute and the inability or unwillingness to do so was a liability. In that context, people found themselves handling emergencies all day and making time for their "real" work late at night, early in the morning, or on weekends. Unscheduled meetings, often after hours, were common. Some people were energized by the continual crises. As one engineer put it, "There's a rush to being out to dinner and having a call come in that you are needed." Yet most also sensed that the environment of constant stress and overwork was counterproductive. This situation had its obvious gender implications, since the women in the group were most committed to invisible work and most conscious of sacrificing the quality of personal life to achieve in this environment.

Based on this feedback, the engineers, the group leader, and the CIAR team sat down to consider work practice changes that might have an effect on the culture of crisis. Someone suggested arbitrarily ending the workday at 5:00 P.M., a step that might force people to plan better in order to get their work done within that time constraint. This idea was met with derision and strong negative reaction by other members of the group. But the lively discussion that ensued got people thinking more creatively about how they spend their time at work. The group worked with these ideas and eventually translated them into an experimental work practice change they called "quiet time"—a period of a few hours during the day set aside for uninterrupted individual work. The idea was that in addition to making it easier for the engineers to get their "real" work done during business hours, this change would help the group with other issues, such as setting priorities and differentiating between unnecessary interruptions and interactions that were essential for coordination and learning. Everybody felt good about the potential benefits of this change.

When it came to planning the change in detail, however, people started to see reasons why it wouldn't work. For example, many people became uncomfortable with the idea that quiet time would be inviolable. They pushed to define the conditions under which it would be OK to interrupt a colleague during those few hours. Eventually, the engineers and the CIAR team came up with the principle that if an issue were important enough to pull someone out of a meeting under normal circumstances, it was important enough to permit breaking quiet time. This solution worked for most people, but the group leader remained unconvinced. The whole pace of product development would slow down significantly, he believed, if engineers couldn't get the help they needed to deal with problems immediately when they arose. He was also concerned that the limit on interactions would undermine his ability to monitor and coordinate work.

Another potential roadblock in the planning of this work practice change was the group leader's concern about how it would affect his ability to supervise and report on the progress of product development. Previously, each subsystem team sent reports to the group leader who worked with his manager to prepare elaborate presentations for review by the vice president. This task took engineers' time, which they felt was unproductive. But using the everyday reports that each team generated routinely seemed dangerous to the group leader because he was afraid that the group would not look professional when upper management made its operational review.

In the end, quiet time could proceed only because it was clearly limited and defined as an experiment. The initial trial set aside three mornings a week for two and a half weeks, after which there would be a review and another decision to proceed. It was also agreed that the group could decide to stop at any time if the change seemed to be undermining its performance. The limited time frame of the experiment made the group leader feel comfortable in negotiating a temporary suspension of the reporting rules for his group, during which time he submitted its ordinary working reports for review.

The quiet-time experiment—which the software group continued for several months—had a number of positive effects. A number of people, including the group leader, spoke enthusiastically of completing tasks during normal working hours that they had previously been forced to do late at night. Quiet time also heightened the group's collective awareness about interaction. Of necessity, they began to set priorities, since they could not interrupt their colleagues at will, and they started to be more comfortable in holding each other to higher standards in this regard—for example, by saying, "I'm busy now. Can we meet later?" In addition, the group leader and the operational review committee learned that using the regular status reports of the subsystem teams had the unanticipated benefit of providing better information because the material, being less processed, was more candid. Far from being derailed by the work–personal life intervention, as the group leader had feared, the team surprised itself and everyone else by launching its new product on time and winning a number of excellence awards.

The software engineering group came away from its quiet-time experiment feeling that it had been successful. Team members' mental models and behavior—around interruptions, supervision by the group leader, and status reports—had clearly shifted in ways that had positive results. Nonetheless, the quiet-time regime did not endure beyond the experimental period of a few months. Though people continued to use their time more effectively during regular working hours, they slipped into using their new "free" time for additional work. The long-term prospects for Dual Agenda change thus remained in doubt.

The CIAR team in this case judged that the next challenges for this group were to devise a new experiment that would push further in legitimating personal-life claims on the time saved by working more efficiently and to come up with ways to acknowledge and encourage the invisible work that could provide a longer-term solution to its perennial state of crisis. In other words, further progress required a reassertion of the equity side of the Dual Agenda. The engineering group would have to take the next step, and the next step after that, in order to turn a small win like the quiet-time experiment into lasting change. The mutual-inquiry approach had worked effectively in the design of the quiet-time experiment, making it possible for concerns and objections to bubble up and receive serious consideration. Going forward, had it been possible to continue the effort, mutual inquiry would have helped this group build on its learning from the initial success—but unfortunately, this did not occur.

Staying with Mutual Inquiry: Midcourse Corrections

The case of the software engineering group brings us back to the central dilemma of the CIAR method: its efficacy depends completely on holding on to *both* parts of the Dual Agenda—equity and effectiveness—yet the greatest resistance *on every level* comes at the point of connection between the two. This is the legacy of the separation of spheres. CIAR researchers need to be prepared to deal with this and can do so by anticipating the need and planning for midcourse corrections in the action phase of a change initiative. This step helps maintain the all-important experimental frame.

Experience has taught us that these midcourse corrections are essential for success, in part because it is simply impossible to design an experiment that anticipates every contingency. Even more important, however, is the need to recognize from the very beginning and to plan for the learning opportunities that can only come in the action phase, as the group works through layers of resistance toward greater understanding of the underlying assumptions it seeks to challenge. This "peeling the onion" experience is a critical part of the implementation process. But it can be difficult to negotiate because much of the learning comes from experiences that feel like failure. Hence advance planning for midcourse corrections is important, psychologically as well as practically.

The members of the CIAR team need to keep in mind and communicate the fact that once the design phase of the experiment is over, the hard work is just beginning. As the experiment proceeds, they need to remind themselves to frame the problems that will inevitably arise as occasions for learning more about the underlying assumptions rather than as reflections of poor design. Otherwise, they and the work group engaged in the action experiment may be unwilling or unprepared to face those problems in a mode of mutual inquiry instead of what one CIAR team member described wistfully as a "ready-made solutions mode."

Some of our learning about the value of midcourse corrections has come the hard way, through projects with disappointing outcomes. For example, in the case of the quiet-time experiment, there was no framework for sustaining mutual inquiry about the implications of dropping the equity part of the Dual Agenda. In that instance, the experiment was set up as a onetime event to test the Dual Agenda concept, not as part of a larger change initiative. When the established cultural norms associated with the underlying assumptions about commitment and competence reasserted themselves, it was difficult for people to acknowledge or push back against them. One CIAR team member who revisited the software engineering group six months after the experiment had ended found that the group's managers had recently reinstituted quiet time in an attempt to get its current project back on track after it had fallen behind schedule. Yet far from embracing the change as before, the engineers were resentful and uncooperative. As one of them stated, "The managers were not taking our interests into account. They were not trying to make life better for us. They were just trying to get whatever productivity enhancements they could. They don't get it. . . . We had no incentive [this time] to abide by quiet time."[5] This story captures an unfortunate missed opportunity and a clear case in which an initial agreement to evaluate results on both dimensions of the Dual Agenda and make needed corrections could have improved the outcome.

Sometimes, however, even agreeing up front is not enough. In Chapter Three, we described a corporate accounting group whose effort to implement a flextime scheme called Coordinated Work Schedules (CWS) floundered because the effectiveness piece of the Dual Agenda fell by the wayside. CWS worked quite well for a couple of months but then broke down rapidly as users began treating it more and more like a benefit, disassociated from work effectiveness concerns. Co-workers shrank from confronting each other about real or perceived abuses, and flextime became a drag on the work group's effectiveness rather than an enhancement.

As the experiment progressed and people began to enjoy the benefits of flexible schedules, they were reluctant to evaluate both sides of the Dual Agenda. When members of the CIAR team called to see how things were going, people were eager to talk about the personal-life improvements but less than eager to complete surveys documenting the impact of CWS on work effectiveness. After the fact, when participants talked frankly with the researchers, they admitted that part of what had held them back from filling out the evaluation surveys was a fear that if work effectiveness outcomes were not showing significant improvement, the experiment might be canceled midstream. Similarly, the managers in the unit recognized the effectiveness problems as they developed but resisted the efforts of the CIAR team to come back on-site for a review in part at least because they didn't want to pronounce CWS a failure and lose the ability to flex occasionally themselves. When the team did return eight months later, it could only be for a "postmortem" review, not the kind of midcourse evaluation that might have made corrections possible.

In this organization, the culture of overwork had been so extreme and so painful, and the hunger for change so great, that people simply could not remain in inquiry mode when it seemed that the flextime experiment was not working as planned. As in the case of the quiet-time experiment, the loss of the experimental frame undercut the possibility for lasting change. The unit abandoned CWS, leaving people feeling disillusioned and putting the Dual Agenda on hold indefinitely.

Taken together, these two cases provide a cautionary tale about the central role of mutual inquiry in Dual Agenda work. Organizations need to be willing to create room for diverse viewpoints and feelings to emerge and to gain recognition, and groups involved in Dual Agenda change work need to have the capacity to engage and work with resistance. Only in this way can they succeed to surface and modify the deeply rooted assumptions that govern work practices and culture in gendered organizations. These conditions are difficult to sustain. But when they are present, the results can be significant.

The Cumulative Power of Small Wins

We do not yet know what gender equity looks like in work organizations—we just have a vision and a concept of how to work toward it. Indeed, on the one hand, it is easy to get discouraged thinking about the vastness of the change we are trying to launch, given the pervasiveness of gendered norms, not just in the world of paid work but in society at large. On the other hand, we see enormous potential in the small-scale changes that Dual Agenda initiatives have produced.

Even in cases like the quiet-time and CWS experiments, in which established assumptions reassert themselves and overwhelm experimental changes in work practices, at least some of the people who participated will carry with them the experience of Dual Agenda change. We should not underestimate the long-term importance of these individual experiences. We know, for example, that the full engagement of managers as well as staff in the CWS experiment and all the work leading up to it created some significant shifts within the organization.

The concept of what people called "reciprocity" entered the culture as a counterweight to the dominant norms that made it very difficult for people to limit the amount of time spent at work. Reciprocity refers to the fact that just as work organizations expect that personal life crises will be kept at a minimum through planning and adequate backup, people should be able to expect the same of the workplace. Bringing such a concept into awareness and discussing it can cause shifts in thinking that have real impact. Sometimes the impact is subtle, perhaps simply offering a language to name something people have experienced individually ("I have to respond to this crisis") as something more systemic ("It is irresponsible to operate continually in crisis mode"). And sometimes the impact is more direct, as in the case we mentioned in Chapter Four of the manager who carried the Dual Agenda concept with him to a new unit because he believed it would help his group be more effective even though there were no obvious work–personal life problems.

In the long run, it will most likely be through individuals who have experienced Dual Agenda changes and who then, like that manager, become seed carriers for the concept that small wins will build to large-scale change. We have already seen the signs of how this can happen, for example, when a group that has worked on Dual Agenda changes feels confident in helping others do the same. Another sign is when people think and talk about issues in new ways, using Dual Agenda concepts to interpret what is going on, and linking equity and effectiveness in their solutions to familiar business problems.

In one manufacturing site, the human resource manager was dealing with a crisis of hiring and retention on one of the lines. She knew that some of the issues had to do with long hours and work–personal life stress and, in response, had tried all the standard policy-level solutions. When she went for advice to her corporate-level manager, that person, who had the experience of coordinating a Dual Agenda project, helped her understand the issue differently. Instead of trying additional policy changes, they decided to undertake a Dual Agenda initiative, linking the workload and overtime issues with effectiveness.

Another positive sign is when changed thinking gets into the ethos, as in the following case of a large organization that had been known as a "non-family-friendly" company before a Dual Agenda change initiative. In a yearlong project, two work units experimented with a variety of work practice changes. This initiative had some local limited impact in the short run, and in the succeeding four years, people who had participated in those experiments helped others launch efforts to make Dual Agenda changes in their own work groups. Now openness to flexibility and other kinds of work practice changes are widespread.

Building on Action Experiments: A Detailed Example

Between the mid-1980s and the mid-1990s, this bank holding company had emerged as one of the largest in the United States, experiencing in the process all of the wrenching changes associated with industry consolidation.[6] These included seventy-five mergers and acquisitions over a ten-year period, followed by reorganizations, substantial downsizing (elimination of six thousand jobs in three years), and implementation of other cost-cutting strategies, for example, relocation of units from urban to suburban office facilities. Going forward, the company faced a number of challenges. In particular, it had problems in the area of customer service; and it had a long way to go to meet a corporate objective of becoming known as an employer of choice.

The chairman and chief executive officer learned about Dual Agenda work and decided to initiate a project, with the idea that it could address both these concerns, among others. He wanted to help employees adjust to the dramatic changes in their work environment, in part by achieving a greater degree of integration between work and personal life. This project was to be a pilot for changes he hoped would ultimately spread throughout the organization.

The CEO assigned responsibility for the Dual Agenda initiative to a senior woman, an executive vice president and director of human resources. She created an internal team to work with the action researchers, who represented an academic research institute that had agreed to partner with the company on this project. Jointly, they selected two sites for CIAR work. One was the reporting and management information systems (MIS) group in the corporate portfolio management unit. The other was a small business loan development unit that had only recently come into existence through the consolidation of a number of underwriting departments and had just moved from a downtown location to a suburban one. At each site, the researchers used a combination of surveys, individual interviews (including spouse interviews), and roundtable discussions to gather data and develop an analysis of underlying assumptions and potential leverage points for change. Then they collaborated with the work groups to design and implement experimental work practice changes, producing some promising results in both cases.

At one site, the change allowed employees to work from home one or two days a week or otherwise flex their hours. The manager herself began telecommuting one day a week, and these scheduling changes had a number of positive effects. Of necessity, the coordination of the subsystems had to be more formalized—something the manager had previously tried to instigate with little success. And flextime and telecommuting, long sought by employees in vain, now became common practice. At the other site, short of staff because of previous reengineering, the bank agreed experimentally to hire temporary clerical staff and to train an administrator to take over some of the work of the underwriters. The underwriters thus had more time available to do the job of underwriting and to do so with less stress. In each case, both work and people's experiences improved.

These Dual Agenda changes were initially framed as experimental pilots for a limited period of time, and turnover in key personnel was a constraint on follow-through. One manager moved on, and the vice president for HR, who had collaborated closely in setting up the pilots, understood the process, and had held the responsibility for diffusing the results in the organization as a whole, assumed a new post. The responsibility for sustaining the work within the company devolved on members of the corporate HR staff. With some consultation from members of the original Dual Agenda research team, they slowly initiated a number of new Dual Agenda projects, what they call "designing work for life" projects. They engaged six work groups in four divisions, roughly two hundred employees in all. While the emphasis in these initiatives was more on increasing productivity than on enabling work–personal life integration, they maintained the basic principle of reciprocity fundamental to the Dual Agenda. The company's self-described approach "looks at the work processes themselves and reengineers them to be less stressful, less time-consuming, and more logically organized, thereby enhancing both the quality of work life and the bottom line." At the end of 2000, two projects had been completed, two were ready to proceed, and two had been truncated because of a merger.[7]

Change diffused in other ways as well. The manager of the reporting and MIS group has become a resource for other work groups around the company seeking to introduce flexible work arrangements. The story is more complicated in the small business loan unit, where the senior manager, who had strongly supported and participated in the Dual Agenda project, retired. His successor was not particularly interested in work–personal life issues and wanted to launch his own change effort, focused mainly on quality methods like continuous improvement. Yet the success of the administrative redeployment experiment—publicized by the CIAR team's report and formally recognized by the CEO—provided concrete evidence of the value of the Dual Agenda approach that was difficult to ignore. Over a period of several years, this manager oversaw a continuous improvement effort focused on computerizing and automating basic underwriting tasks. The resulting increase in productivity allowed the unit to enlarge the volume of loans it handled while reducing its head count. Some of the gain, however, was shared with employees. In practical terms, for most people this meant working ten hours a day instead of twelve—not as much of a change as many people would like, but still significant in this industry environment.

Also important, the manager talked about the change in a way that honors the principle of reciprocity: "We wanted to make sure that this was a win/win situation . . . and that was a totally new thing for [the company]. We had never done it before and we are still challenged by it. But it has worked out pretty well, and people actually appear to be happier. They work fewer hours, their productivity is up, and our division is enjoying the benefits."[8]

Conclusion

Action experiments play a critical role in CIAR, enabling people to experience for themselves what it feels like to work in new ways. More than anything else in the method, it is this firsthand experience that makes the Dual Agenda proposition that equity and effectiveness can be mutually supporting, not antithetical, begin to be believable. To achieve these results, CIAR researchers need to engage, legitimate, and work with the resistances that will inevitably arise as people peel back the layers of deeply held assumptions that hold the old, suboptimal ways of working in place. Creating a framework of experimentation for work practice changes and sustaining a mode of mutual inquiry as the experiment proceeds—including anticipating the need for midcourse corrections—are the CIAR tools that support working with resistance in this way.

In our experience with CIAR so far, we have witnessed changes that were dramatically successful but short-lived, though with some effects that played out over time in subtle ways. And we have seen how, as in the case of the banking company described in this chapter, small-scale changes can have a cumulative impact. In Chapter Seven, we take up the question of what CIAR researchers can do to influence these longer-term outcomes. Next, however, we conclude our presentation of the CIAR method with a discussion in Chapter Six of how action research teams, like the organizations they study and seek to change, wrestle with the gendered assumptions and norms that pervade our work cultures.

CHAPTER 6

Walking the Talk: Reflections from the CIAR Team

As we have used Collaborative Interactive Action Research (CIAR) in organizations, trying to create change toward greater equity, we have learned a great deal about what this change entails. We try to model in research teams what we hope to help create: equitable work groups and an environment that supports work–personal life integration. In doing so, we have personally experienced the difficulties involved. Uncovering deeply held assumptions about competence, commitment, and gender—necessary in this endeavor—creates complicated reactions that, if not worked through, can derail change. On many occasions, struggling to put into practice the ideal of an equitable work group, we realized that masculine gendered assumptions shape our own attitudes toward paid work and that challenging them taps into deep issues of identity. Attempting to model what we are striving to achieve with organizations helps us make explicit, both to ourselves and to our organizational partners, our understanding of what this work entails. It is for this reason that we wish to share these reflections on our experiences in CIAR teams with readers who may be contemplating using this method.

The Role of the CIAR Team

Organizations wanting to undertake Dual Agenda change—that is, change aimed at increasing both equity and effectiveness—may naturally ask why they should bring in a team of outsiders to help. Our answer is that trying to create this type of change completely from within a group is particularly difficult: insiders cannot help being caught up in the accepted beliefs, norms, and power dynamics of the group, whereas the essence of Dual Agenda change lies in challenging those beliefs and norms.

We have found in our teams that we ourselves benefit from an outsider who works with us in an analogous way to what we do with organizations, helping us identify our assumptions and see whether we are headed down a wrong path. This person, well versed in this kind of work, kept up with our efforts in the organization but did not join us in the field. There are many parallels between the way this "inside outsider" functions in a CIAR team and the interaction of the team with an organization. Though it is possible that the inside outsider role will not always be necessary in CIAR teams, it has made a significant contribution to the development of the method so far. It is a role we cannot easily replicate from the inside.

People may also ask why the CIAR method calls for the action researcher (or outsider) role of a Dual Agenda change initiative to be filled by more than one person, that is, by a team. As a matter of principle, this fits with our emphasis on collaborative work, as opposed to individual heroics. On the practical side, we have found that on those few occasions when only one of us was involved in an interaction with an organization, we were less successful in dealing with the resistances and challenges that typically emerge in doing this work. Important elements of the situation are also more easily missed with only one person. Finally, CIAR involves a broad range of tasks—interviewing, facilitation, data collection, analysis, presentation, intervention, implementation, and more. It calls for a breadth of skills and knowledge (not to mention time and energy) that one individual alone can hardly be expected to supply. Organizational insiders need to be involved. They are the critical participants in many of those tasks. But the outsider role, to be played effectively, requires a diversity of talents and perspectives that only a team can provide.

Finally, the action research team plays a valuable role as a research instrument. This is true in a general sense when, as we described, the team tries to model the behaviors it advocates and must struggle with its own points of resistance. In addition, we have learned that the CIAR team will often begin to reflect what is going on in the organization in its own dynamics. When team members recognize this phenomenon—usually with the benefit of the inside outsider's perspective—they are able to empathize more fully with people in the organization and provide a more insightful and useful analysis.

Team Makeup and Dynamics

Diversity in team composition is what makes collaboration both worthwhile and challenging, and working effectively with diversity is naturally a high priority, given our equity agenda, both for ourselves and for our organizational partners. In principle, it is important that our teams reflect the gender, racial, and ethnic diversity of the twenty-first-century workplace and model equitable, collaborative relationships within that context. In actuality, we have been largely unsuccessful in creating such teams. On the whole, our teams have had some racial and ethnic diversity, though not as much as would be optimal. But we have found it particularly difficult to attract men to this endeavor, and in one case a man initially interested in joining the project was put off by the demands the team seemed to be making on the style of his participation. Since we are fundamentally concerned with the gendered nature of organizations and of people's perceptions, this is a significant lack.

What are the implications of all-women teams for this work? Since we are women, we may not be able to gauge fully the effect of this pattern. For many of us, coming from male-dominated environments, being on an all-women team is one of the joys of this work. It is easier than in our home environments to establish the quality of relationships we want, and the absence of the gender issues we so typically confront is certainly welcome. All of us bring to our work a clear understanding and experience of many gender inequities, which makes it relatively easy to spot such inequities in our partner organizations. Nonetheless, this homogeneity precludes a type of mutual learning across the sexes that is crucial to our goals and that our organizational partners have to deal with. It is the primary way we have not been able to model a diverse but equitable work group.

In other ways, however, our teams are diverse on many dimensions that are also relevant to workplace dynamics—for example, position, training, skills, age, experience, temperament, personal style, and family situation. We did not handle all of our diversity issues effectively, but in every instance they enriched our understanding of the challenges that diversity presents. And this learning has helped us in our interactions with our organizational partners.

Our view of teams is colored by relational theory, which values mutuality and growth in connection with others.[1] Working in this way challenges one to be authentic in the moment, vulnerable (in the sense of being willing to bring one's own thoughts and uncertainties into the conversation), open to hearing what others have to say and empathic toward the feelings they express, and committed to growing together. Jean Baker Miller and Irene Stiver provide five indicators of when such growth in connection is occurring: feelings of zest, empowered action, new knowledge, a sense of worth for every team member, and a desire for more connection.[2]

Alertness to these indicators helps a team stay on track. When the zest is deflated and the team feels deenergized, it is likely that connection has broken down and the effectiveness of the team will be diminished. One CIAR team, for example, which started out meeting all five conditions, slowly lost them when two members were unable to resolve their feelings of competitiveness. The undercurrent of conflict between them significantly reduced the overall smooth functioning of the team.

In some ways, it is easier to be open to learning from and being influenced by our organizational partners than to practice what we call fluid expertise within the team. Competition may be the major source of this difficulty, especially in teams that include academics, who are grounded in an environment in which individual output is uniquely valued. But tendencies toward hierarchy and control also undermine fluid expertise. It is an effort, therefore—but an important one—to model acceptance of one's own limitations and acknowledgment of other team members' expertise and to accept that reliance on one or the other must shift back and forth as the occasion demands. Struggling to do so has helped us recognize the difficulty as well as the necessity for dealing with diversity in this way.

The Team as a Research Instrument

Team dynamics provide opportunities for learning and knowledge creation because the people on CIAR teams are invariably grappling with many of the same difficult work issues as people in our partnering organizations—for example, issues involving collaboration, diversity, equity, and work–personal life integration. One can also expect in action research that the outside team will at times inadvertently take on the behavior patterns of the organization it is working with. This phenomenon can create some real difficulties but when recognized can also be a source of insight. It is also critically important to be aware of the team's power to influence the organization as the work proceeds, through micro-interventions and feedback and even in more casual interactions. These are facts of life in CIAR teams, and it is best to be explicit and purposeful about using the team's experience as a key element of the research method.

One particularly striking way in which the team serves as a research instrument is when people find themselves reproducing the practices of the organization with which they are partnering. By recognizing what is happening and reflecting on the feelings it generates, the research team learns to appreciate, on a more immediate, emotional level, the issues facing its organizational partners. For example, in one organizational setting, team members found themselves agreeing to an expansion of the project beyond what they had planned for, which created great feelings of pressure. The realization that they were agreeing because not doing so might put their commitment in question was powerful evidence of what was happening in the organization that was putting such stress on its employees. The organizational norms were influencing the research team and its behavior, just as they influenced organizational members themselves.

At another site where great emphasis was placed on always having the correct information, the research team began subtly to change its way of working by acting more expert than its members really were about certain technical matters. The culture of the organization began to silence the research team members. They began to feel that their competence was in doubt if they did not have all the answers, which of course is quite opposite to the notion of fluid expertise that underlies the CIAR method. This experience helped them empathize more fully with the people in that organization and made them realize how difficult the changes they were asking the organization to make in order to meet the Dual Agenda really were. Even more telling was the way, in another setting, the team reproduced a complicated divide within the organization by the way it presented the feedback data, classifying people into professional and nonprofessional categories, and thereby reinforcing a number of existing tensions in the organization. And in yet another instance, the team found itself talking less and less about gender, reflecting the silencing of gender in the organization it was working with.

Though these examples may sound obvious after the fact, in each case it took time for the team to realize what was happening, and it was at such points that the inside outsider was particularly helpful. Just as in the organization itself, the team became subject to the unspoken and unrecognized assumptions and norms prevalent in the situation. Such a process has some similarities to the transference and countertransference in psychotherapy.

Underlying all these cases is the team's attempt to model the norms and work practices it is hoping the organization will adopt. One team, for example, near the end of a multiyear project, reflected on its efforts to create a team culture that supported work–personal life integration. The team had begun with a discussion in which individual team members spoke about their personal values and the boundaries they wanted to set around their personal and professional lives. This led to an agreement to take collective responsibility for getting the work done, reallocating assignments when necessary to support each other's needs for personal time. The group made a point of repeating this discussion when new members joined the team. It followed through on the commitment to respond flexibly to individual situations, for example, by avoiding scheduling meetings at times when a parent with a young child had difficulty attending, and by respecting the wishes of some team members for strict observance of the Sabbath, including no work communication and no travel. Over the course of the project, the team concluded, this behavior created an atmosphere of trust and supportiveness and made it possible to work productively as a group while responding to individuals' personal concerns.

On reflection, however, this team recognized that it had not addressed some underlying assumptions that worked against its efforts to create a culture in which people successfully integrated work and personal life. One was the feeling that some personal-life issues, such as parenting responsibilities or religious beliefs, were more appropriate to bring into the work group than others, such as stress over marital problems. Another was a demanding work ethic that made it difficult to establish and stick to manageable meeting agendas and work plans. By facing these aspects of its own behavior, the team gained greater insight into the barriers to work–personal life integration in its partner organization.

Finally, one example makes it particularly clear how the team itself is subject to the same underlying assumptions it is trying to uncover with its organizational partners. In one of our projects, with a distant organization, the issue arose whether adding a site visit just prior to the official feedback would be useful. When one team member suggested skipping the trip, others almost instinctively interpreted this as signifying that she was considering her own needs and not the quality of the work. This ready assumption that the need to put boundaries on individual time reflects a lack of commitment initially got in the way of thinking how the goal of the trip—to get input on our analysis from our collaborators on site—might be accomplished in another, less time-intensive way. In the end, we did find an alternative, which actually turned out to be more effective. We ourselves had fallen into the same mode of thinking we had been working so hard to overcome in the organization. It was a powerful lesson that helped us be more empathic toward and more effective with our organizational partners.

Working with Resistance: The Other Side of the Equation

Because of the resistance that Dual Agenda change invariably provokes, we have had to learn to deal with attacks on our work in organizations. Both in the field and among ourselves, we have not always reacted constructively to such attacks. Here again, our team experiences have helped deepen our understanding of the CIAR method.

In the field, we know ideally how to respond to hostility or attack. We know such negative reactions are often a form of resistance that provides useful data. We also know that in most cases, the best response is one of inquiry: an expression of interest followed by probing to understand the concern. But team members are human, and when we felt attacked, we sometimes reacted by assuming an expert posture or resorting to other defensive means. We believe in "fluid expertise" and an appropriate mix of advocacy and inquiry, but sometimes we confused the two, explaining our position when what was needed was gentle inquiry to elucidate the other's concern. At other times, we inquired gently only to feel later that we had missed a chance to do what we on the team called "push-backs"—microinterventions aimed at creating opportunities for reframing issues by introducing our own perspective and values. So the judgment of how to handle attacks is complicated, quite apart from the understandable emotional reaction. Nevertheless, when such an event occurs, the team members involved often experience it as "failure."

These situations present special challenges for the team because typically only some members of the team participate in each field engagement. Yet the team as a whole must try to understand and analyze their experience. So what happens when these members come back to a team meeting to report? Again, the appropriate response is to work with the team members involved, to empathize with their feelings and help them understand their own reactions, and jointly to figure out ways to reinforce the inquiry mode in such situations in the future. The team should also work together to grasp the meaning of the resistance or response by the organizational members, which is central to understanding the organization. But this has not always happened. Rather, on more than one occasion, we have found ourselves blaming the people involved for their "ineptitude."

For example, in one Dual Agenda project, contrary to our usual guidelines, one team member went alone to a preliminary explanatory session at a site. It turned into an unpleasant attack on the team member, and the exchange set back our relations with the partner organization. Initially we blamed the individual for not handling the situation properly, creating unpleasant and unproductive dynamics in the team. Only much later, when it became clear that the organization's reaction reflected an internal battle that had nothing to do with the action research project, were we able to clear away the bad feelings that resulted.

In another situation, two team members spent a whole day on-site doing team building, "enabler and barrier" analysis, and other such interventionist exercises. When they reported on this activity, it seemed that they had made no progress toward defining an action step that would meet the Dual Agenda—the stated purpose of the site visit. The rest of the team, mostly academics, could not understand why such a day had been "wasted," and an uncomfortable meeting ensued. Again, it was only some time later that it became clear how important that day was for the eventual success of the project at that particular site. We realized that the interventionists had sensed in the work group a lack of readiness to proceed to the action step and by taking the time to deal with it had cleared the way for the group to embrace change more enthusiastically later on.

So what can one learn from these experiences? First, if one responds to resistance or attack by organizational members with defensive or expert reactions, the effort will be set back. Second, it is best always to have at least two team members onsite to maximize the probability of picking up the right cues and to minimize the possibility of reacting inappropriately. Finally, second-guessing in the analysis of these events by the whole team is counterproductive. Instead, team members need to engage the on-site experience in the same inquiry mode we employ with our organizational partners.

Conclusion

We have shared in this chapter our learning about how difficult it is to create equitable dynamics in work groups, even when, as in our case, this is part of a shared purpose. Any team considering taking up Dual Agenda work needs to be prepared to face these challenges. At the same time, we have suggested that the struggle to "walk our talk" has strengthened our ability to support our organizational partners in a variety of ways, for example, by helping us get better at modeling the behavior that Dual Agenda change entails and by providing insight into organizational cultures through their effects on our own team interactions. Organizations need outsiders to support these difficult change efforts, but in particular they need people who are open to wrestling with Dual Agenda issues in their own lives and work.

Our final reflection is on the need to allow time for reflection, which is an essential part of Dual Agenda work and not merely an add-on to the "real" work. As essential as this activity is, however, we often find ourselves lacking the time to do it properly or to do it at all. Invariably, some of the most difficult issues in a Dual Agenda project revolve around limited resources of time and energy in the CIAR team. What we can see, from a distance, is that we have exacerbated this problem through the same kinds of behavior we observe in the organizations we study: for example, working harder, not smarter, or throwing time at problems indiscriminately rather than setting priorities. Of course, our behavior is part of a larger social pattern, which is one more challenge for Dual Agenda teams trying to walk their talk.

PART 3

Looking Ahead

CHAPTER 7

Sustaining and Diffusing Equitable Change

The chapters in Part Two outlined the Collaborative Interactive Action Research (CIAR) method for creating Dual Agenda change in work practices at a local site. Determining how to sustain and diffuse such change is one of the biggest challenges. Our goal for diffusion is to create momentum for advancing gender equity, including work–personal life integration, both within and outside the specific groups we work with. Ideally, this means that a critical mass of the organization's members need to believe that it is both possible and appropriate to give serious consideration to equity issues in the work setting and that doing so can lead to improved performance. That is, they need to understand and take up the Dual Agenda. And they need to have a way to achieve Dual Agenda outcomes. Thus one of the things most important to diffuse is a working knowledge of and experience with CIAR itself.[1]

As already indicated, CIAR is an emergent method, and diffusion is the area in which it is least well developed. There have been some successes, but a great deal of our learning has come from frustration and failure. Taking both together, however, we have begun to identify factors that either promote or hinder diffusion objectives, as well as some steps that action researchers can take to help it along.[2]

Diffusion: From Day One and Throughout

It is necessary to keep diffusion issues in mind from the very beginning of a Dual Agenda project and to be conscious of opportunities to promote diffusion throughout. At the level of project planning, this means holding on to an understanding of the need for senior management participation as one negotiates the terms of engagement with an organization. It also means developing strategies for cultivating and working with internal change agents and for attaining a critical mass of supporters of change. At the level of execution, it means recognizing that each phase of a CIAR project holds significant diffusion possibilities.

It is important, for example, to keep in mind that every individual interview is an opportunity for micro-intervention. It is during these one-on-one interactions that people first make Dual Agenda connections on a personal level. On the one hand, they begin to see systemic explanations for personal experiences. On the other hand, and equally important, they often begin to see how their own assumptions and actions support the systemic pattern. Those insights are the foundation for individual change and influence, which lays the groundwork for broader acceptance later on. In addition, since individuals make up supportive constituencies, they are also essential for lasting systemic change.

The iterative aspect of CIAR is a further aid to diffusion. As a Dual Agenda analysis begins to emerge, it is fed back for collaborative inquiry not only in formal sessions but also in each succeeding individual interview or group session. As more and more people work with it, understanding and ownership of the new narrative spreads, and it gains credibility and force. CIAR team members and internal change agents need to keep diffusion in mind as they think about who should attend feedback sessions, briefings, roundtables, and so forth — understanding the need to broaden continually the circle of people engaged in the process.

As a project moves to the action experiment stage, the presence of a broad constituency that is aware of and understands Dual Agenda work can help sustain the experimental group. Change can proceed on an informal basis outside the pilot group as a result of that awareness. At the same time, members of experimental teams can be effective agents of diffusion by spreading the word of successful outcomes to action experiments and thus can stimulate interest in expanding Dual Agenda work. But it is important that communication about CIAR projects report not only concrete results but also the thinking behind them and the way mind-sets changed in order to make them work.

What other work groups need to reproduce is the process by which those changes emerged. CIAR researchers can provide support for group members to share this aspect of their experience with the larger organization, which may be indifferent or hostile to Dual Agenda concepts.

As a Dual Agenda initiative proceeds, perhaps the biggest challenge diffusion poses is that it takes a great deal of time. In their early planning, action researchers and the organization need to develop a strategy for diffusion that takes into account the time for activities such as keeping in touch, following up inquiries for others in the organization, and communicating results. Timing is also important, but often it is impossible for action researchers from the outside to be as opportunistic as the fluid situation inside an organization demands, so moments for diffusion are lost. Serendipity plays a role, but planning that anticipates contingencies can also help.

In 1997, the Center for Gender in Organizations at Simmons Graduate School of Management held a case conference on "scaling up" Dual Agenda change. Participants defined scaling up as "moving gender from the margins to the mainstream and moving from organizational experiments to institutionalized alternative work practices." They suggested that the best, and perhaps only, hope for sustained change may be pressure brought to bear by external forces.[3] The quality movement in U.S. manufacturing provides an example. In that case, in company after company, an extended top-down effort in response to pressure from competitors did, indeed, drive diffusion of fundamental change. But even under those conditions, the effort to diffuse a new way of working throughout a large organization required an enormous amount of effort and time. It took Xerox almost ten years, starting in the early 1980s, to combat Japanese competition by infusing the principles of total quality management throughout the company, even with a concerted top-down campaign.[4] And it would probably take even longer to have such a positive result in the area of gender equity and work–personal life integration. Nonetheless, it is important for Dual Agenda teams to plan for diffusion, remembering, though, that it will take persistence and patience.

What to Diffuse? Linking Product to Process

CIAR interventions are site-specific, and action experiments that are successful in one setting cannot be relied on to be effective at another site. It is tempting, after a successful intervention, to take an innovative work practice and simply import it into other groups. For example, the success of the software engineering group described in Chapter Five inspired other engineering groups in the same company to adopt quiet time at their own sites. But they did not go through the process that had produced the quiet-time idea, and the experiments did not work. Deborah Kolb and Deborah Merrill-Sands shed light on this problem, reporting on similar results in work on gender equity with the agricultural research institute that we described in Chapter Three.[5] In this organization, too, long hours of work and time famine were significant Dual Agenda issues. The scientists decided to try the quiet-time experiment, not because it had emerged from their own Dual Agenda work, but because they had read of its successful implementation by the software engineers. Here, too, the experiment failed to take hold.

Quiet time provided a solution in the software engineering group because both managers and engineers recognized that an essential step in moving out of a continual-crisis mode was to begin to distinguish between "unnecessary interruptions and interactions that are essential for learning and coordination."[6] The agricultural research organization was also struggling with a crisis mentality, but the source of its time famine related less to interruptions than to workloads that had gotten out of hand as the organization's priorities shifted. "The goal of quiet time was to protect time during the normal work day for researchers and administrative staff to do their primary work," write Kolb and Merrill-Sands. "What was not addressed was the volume and pace of work. . . . Nor did [this organization] try an experiment that could challenge the cultural contradictions [between existing norms and emerging priorities] that were creating the time problem in the first place."[7]

The lesson we draw is that diffusion does not mean taking over the concrete outcome — the product or the solution — of a Dual Agenda experiment. Rather, the CIAR *process*, by which one uncovers the forces that operate on the surface and beneath it, needs to diffuse. At the intersection of organizational culture and work practices are critical differences, even among apparently similar organizations, that make direct transfer of successful experiments from one site to another problematic, if not impossible. To avoid becoming just another "flavor of the month" change initiative, an experimental change in work practice must be closely and explicitly linked to the underlying assumptions it seeks to challenge. That linkage is not readily transferable — it needs to be experienced — and has to emerge organically from the CIAR process.

Innovations in this area arise from collective shifts in mindset — changes without which it would be difficult or impossible to work through the resistances that inevitably occur. And so when groups achieve success, it is not only the particular new work practice but the collaborative inquiry by which it was produced that provide the conviction and energy required to make change happen and to sustain and renew it as necessary.

The same principle applies to another key product of Dual Agenda projects—the analysis. A cultural analysis (or narrative) that rings true for people across an organization and that reframes organizational issues in helpful ways can be a powerful force for change.[8] But there is a danger, also, that it may become merely a collection of catchy phrases that lack motivating force and provide little insight.

For example, Ann Rippin describes the case of a consumer products manufacturer and retailer for which a Dual Agenda team developed a cultural analysis based on extensive one-on-one interviewing, observation, and review of documents. The analysis described how a systemic lack of clarity around critical work issues—time, roles, and authority—created a "cycle of incompetence" that affected everyone in the company, but women most severely. Work with this analysis had a profound impact on two participants in a feedback session with a group of "high-flying young managers." One was the head of national retail operations. "He heard the story as a way of reassuring himself that he 'wasn't going mad,' that the dysfunction that he was caught up in was systemic rather than individual, and that there was a way to break out of the pattern," writes Rippin. He arranged for a feedback session for his regional sales managers, and they in turn took up the story as "a way of challenging what [was] happening around them, independently of any consultant." The company's general manager for product development, a woman, also gained important insight from the feedback session and analysis. "She saw in the story an explanation of why she could not do her job properly and went on to use it to disrupt the self-defeating cycle of competence and incompetence we had identified. She described to me how she used it as a lens to examine her own management decisions, as well as a way of calling a halt to the cycle and thus breaking out of it."[9]

Those examples show how both the vision and the energy for change can flow from a Dual Agenda analysis. In contrast, Rippin describes how some of the vocabulary of the analysis spread rapidly throughout the company and took on a life of its own, apart from the CIAR process: "It was like letting a genie out of a bottle." The analysis had described two common, and gendered, strategies for functioning within the corporate culture. One was heroics; the other was building, which the team pointed out was invisible work. "Suddenly everyone seemed to be talking to us about their jobs in terms of heroics. Everyone seemed to be looking for evidence that they were doing invisible work. . . . People used the vocabulary and in using it, and appearing proficient in using it (e.g., we must respect and reward invisible work), could effectively avoid doing anything about it."[10] Detached from the collaborative inquiry process and experienced as sound bites or slogans, the analysis lost its capacity to stimulate Dual Agenda change.

These cases suggest again that it is the process as much as any specific, concrete results that must diffuse. Without process understanding, the will and the capacity for pursuing Dual Agenda work are likely to dissipate, even in the face of a compelling analysis or in the wake of a clearly successful pilot project. Conversely, when a sufficiently large subset of an organization has participated in the collaborative inquiry process and has had the experience of CIAR, both collectively and individually, such a group can sustain momentum for change, even when particular action experiments are not demonstrably successful.

Attaining a Critical Mass:
Large- and Small-Scale Interventions

Does diffusion of Dual Agenda work throughout an organization require that every unit work with outside consultants or action researchers in the CIAR mode? The answer is no, but there must be enough people—a critical mass—who both embrace the Dual Agenda and have some experience in the method to push the work forward. The positive value of having a large portion of an organization participate in the collaborative inquiry process cannot be overstated.

For example, in the agricultural research organization they worked with, Kolb and Merrill-Sands conducted individual interviews with about one-fourth of the 120 professional scientists and support staff and then presented their analysis to the entire organization. In addition to discussion in the feedback session, the organization's staff had the opportunity to react to and discuss the researchers' findings in smaller groups, at roundtable discussions. Quiet time was only one of a number of experimental changes in work practices to come out of those roundtables. As already noted, that experiment did not take: few researchers or support staff members chose to observe quiet time, and almost none did so consistently. Yet surprisingly, after eighteen months, the "unsuccessful" experiment seemed to have shifted both attitudes and behavior around the use of time and time issues in the organization. In the words of Kolb and Merrill-Sands:

> Many [staff members] argued that quiet time played an important role in legitimating staffs' right to raise the issue of time pressures and to assert control over their own time. . . . The [organization's] researchers

began to . . . bound the time they were willing to give to the organization. . . . Similarly, the administrative staff began to "push back" on last-minute requests and demands and began to challenge the work behaviors that contributed to crisis management. . . . Indeed, the volume of work and the cultural assumptions that drove it were now on the table in a way that had failed to happen at the time of the initial intervention.[11]

Five years after the initial interviewing and feedback, change continued in this organization. In particular, senior managers began to give support to the development of work plans that accounted realistically for time requirements, a proposal they had resisted when it surfaced in the roundtables, "because they were afraid it would compromise productivity and quality and would have consequences for funding." In speculating on the sources of this sustained momentum for change, Kolb and Merrill-Sands emphasize the groundwork that had been laid in the initial CIAR interaction. They had presented an analysis, based on individual interviews, that identified underlying assumptions shaping work practices with some negative consequences for both organizational effectiveness and gender equity. "We spent a great deal of time with individuals and groups, working through the analysis," they note. "It was clear in the feedback session that staff at all levels connected with the cultural analysis. What they were not ready to do at that time was experiment in ways that would seriously challenge [the underlying] assumptions. That took time, and over time, other things happened that made change more of a possibility."[12]

Two key things that happened, according to Kolb and Merrill-Sands, were the rise and gradual expansion of a constituency committed to change and the personal experience of time problems by more and more people, including senior managers, in their own workloads and schedules. Critical to both those developments, the researchers suggest, was a widely shared understanding of the Dual Agenda analysis, which offered a convincing narrative to explain the collective experience in this organization. The narrative provided a context within which time problems came to be viewed as systemic as well as individual and the desire for change increasingly appeared both legitimate and appropriate. Significant changes took shape as individuals at all levels of the hierarchy—in particular, senior research fellows and managers—began to reinterpret their personal experiences within that context. Finally, all of this happened with minimal outside intervention after the original CIAR work.

This case illustrates how the power of a Dual Agenda analysis (or narrative) to effect change is directly related to the extent to which the collaborative inquiry that produces it engages a critical mass within the organization. Merrill-Sands and colleagues provide a confirming case, based on work with another center. For that seven-hundred-person organization, they designed a process "to lay a foundation for diffusion," interviewing extensively and conducting a weeklong feedback in both plenary and small group sessions, as well as preview and wrap-up meetings with senior managers and a gender task force. "A large number of people in the organization were exposed to the analysis, worked with and developed it, and participated in generating ideas for action steps and change experiments," they write. "The mental models [described in the analysis] provided handles with which staff could keep assumptions explicit and sustain awareness and discourse on how the mental models are affecting decisions, behaviors, and values. This clearly had an impact on individuals' daily work practices, behaviors, and interactions."[13]

Over a period of several years, the action researchers assert, this collective experience also produced significant changes in organizationwide systems and practices—for example, improved communication between senior management and staff, more attention to team training, and development of a protocol for 360-degree performance evaluations that recognized much of what had been invisible work. All of these changes explicitly targeted issues of equity and effectiveness.

To be sure, both of these organizations are relatively small and relatively flat, with hundreds, not thousands, of employees. And they are more stable in personnel than for-profit companies in highly competitive industries tend to be. So the learning from CIAR work was not as quickly lost. The logistical difficulty of engaging a critical mass of people in a very large organization with high turnover is of course much greater. Nevertheless, these cases provide a useful model for how to create a context for broad diffusion of Dual Agenda change.

In theory, within such a context, the cumulative experience of experimental changes in work practices (undertaken at the work group level) could build into lasting, dramatic change—as in the total quality revolution. In practice, so far, we have not succeeded in bringing such large-scale and small-scale change together. The case of the banking institution described in Chapter Five suggests that a number of successful work group experiments can contribute to a shift in the organizational ethos so that other work groups feel encouraged and empowered to try making Dual Agenda change. In that case, though under an umbrella of top management support but without the context of broad participation in examining underlying assumptions, the unfolding of change in the bank will necessarily be slow and piecemeal. Conversely, in cases where broad participation in CIAR interviews, feedback, and discussion have created a context for systemwide change but the initiative has stopped short of getting down to local-level work, the change process has also been incomplete. One of the big challenges remaining in developing the CIAR method, therefore, is to develop a diffusion strategy that brings the two—large-scale and small-scale change work—together.

Internal Change Agents

There are, of course, various ways in which insiders act as organizational change agents. Some individuals or groups are assigned the role, either as part of a job description or within the context of a specific project. Other people take it on without a formal charge as they become committed to changing the system or perhaps just to doing things differently in their own spheres of activity. Speaking or acting individually or in concert, those people play an essential role in diffusion, acting as a constituency in support of change.

For example, in one organization, action researchers worked jointly with a work-life committee that had been established prior to the start of the Dual Agenda project. The leader of that group, a gifted instinctive change agent, translated the analysis that emerged from the CIAR process into models of change that she took, with success, to the highest levels of the division. In another instance, the CIAR team actually set up a committee to work with, and the committee's input and impact on the organization as a whole were crucial to successful Dual Agenda change. These successes flowed from a collaborative, interactive exchange. The research team worked closely with the internal committee throughout the project, and in this process the internal change agents became the bearers of the understanding that provided the impetus for change.

A different and more pedagogical approach to the problem of how to engage internal change agents in the effort has also arisen in Dual Agenda work. Its centerpiece is an elegant conceptual framework that explicates the theory of gendered organizations and the principle of working at the level of underlying assumptions to effect Dual Agenda changes.[14] This approach raises questions, because it is based on a very different kind of exchange: it is more a teacher-to-student exchange, while CIAR is self-consciously undidactic. Based on our experience in projects of this type, we now believe that collaborative inquiry is an important tool in this change work and that cognitive learning alone is unlikely to prepare internal change agents to use a method that involves uncovering issues that operate on noncognitive levels.

Evidence from the field suggests that some connection, through personal experience, to both the issues and the CIAR method is important for people to be willing and able to push this difficult work forward from the inside. But there is also evidence that the process can be transferred to others in the organization with only minimal outside help. CIAR researchers are unlikely to be around as the diffusion process plays out in an organization. They will have to hand off the work to internal change agents at some point, though possibly maintaining some contact on an "as needed" basis. Learning how to make this transfer efficiently is a critical challenge for future development of CIAR.

In the case of people who emerge spontaneously as informal change agents, the challenge is not one of preparation but of support. A goal of the CIAR team should be to have at the end of a project an internal constituency holding on to the Dual Agenda narrative and perhaps challenging the status quo in various ways. The team can promote diffusion by devising ways to give that group a voice, for example, by planning a follow-up round of interviews and feedback.

However they take up the role, internal change agents face tremendous hurdles, the most significant of which is that they operate within the power structure of the system they are trying to change. Practically speaking, this means that internal change agents will, consciously or unconsciously, feel the need to balance the agenda for change against the priorities imposed by the organization. Opportunities will be missed; momentum will ebb and flow; change agents will move on. Those who stay will likely need encouragement and assistance from the outside—in dealing with resistance, in keeping the attention and support of management, and more fundamentally, in holding on to the Dual Agenda. This is another way in which promoting diffusion requires patience and long-term commitment, as well as advance planning, by the CIAR team.

The Role of Leadership

Leadership of a Dual Agenda initiative by top management is no "silver bullet" that can effect change by itself. Deeply held assumptions are not susceptible to change by executive order. At the same time, leadership, positional or not, is often essential to move work groups toward change. Cultivating and supporting leadership at all levels is a vital diffusion issue.

Nonetheless, it is a fact of life in most work organizations that senior managers carry more weight than others. And they can bring a unique and necessary perspective to collaborative inquiry. Having them personally involved is therefore extremely valuable, though it is often difficult to achieve. Even when they approve Dual Agenda change work in their organizations, senior managers often do not perceive gender equity and work–personal life integration as issues relevant to their own work domains, specifically to the formation and pursuit of organizational strategy. Individuals who have risen to the top in the existing system can, understandably, have difficulty seeing the need for challenging it in fundamental ways. However, in the few cases where it has been possible to enlist senior management to engage in this process, results have been better sustained.

Individual Change at the Top: A Detailed Example

In Chapter Three, we described a Dual Agenda change in a three-hundred-person customer administration unit. An experiment allowing work groups to take control of their own schedules successfully addressed the work–personal life issue of inflexibility and the performance issue of top-down control getting in the way of implementing self-directed teams. Delving deeper into this case provides an illuminating example of individual change at the top of an organization and its impact.

The initiative in this particular unit was part of a broader effort to understand why employees were only minimally using a wide array of flexible work options offered by the company, which had a reputation for leadership in the area of employee benefits. The unit's leader was a reluctant participant in the Dual Agenda project. He had enjoyed considerable success thus far by taking a conservative approach in matters of organizational change, adopting new ideas only once they had been tested by others. At the same time, he did have a business problem related to work–personal life conflict: a high level of absenteeism and lateness among frontline employees who dealt directly with customers, mainly by phone, was making it difficult for the unit to achieve its goals for customer service and satisfaction.

As a CIAR team worked with this unit to examine its work practices through the lens of work–personal life integration, it uncovered some underlying assumptions about the necessity for hierarchy and control. In brief, these were that excellent performance required energetic top-down direction and that "driving the business need" meant keeping close control over most aspects of how the work got done. These assumptions had clear Dual Agenda implications.

On the work–personal life side, the assumptions shaped the unit's implementation of the company's flexibility benefits in such a way as to make it both severely limited in scope and unfair in practical application. The manager of each work group was empowered to grant individual requests for flexibility, based on "need" and dependent on demonstrating that performance would not suffer. Managers tended to see "need" most often in cases of women with children; and they tended to deny or "pocket veto" proposals for flexible arrangements in favor of what people called "jiggling" the system to help individuals out on an ad hoc basis. At the same time, the managers themselves rarely used the benefit of flexibility because they saw it as detrimental to their careers—a sign that they were less than fully committed to ensuring the performance of their groups. The result was that despite having an array of flexibility benefits on the books, this organization was filled with people who were struggling to manage work–personal life conflicts. Discouraged from attempting to address those issues through the system, they were "managing" them on their own—by coming late to work or missing work altogether when they had to.

The CIAR analysis suggested that the same assumptions undermining the intent of flexible work options were also operating to "disempower" workers in the new team structure. Group managers remained accountable for performance and continued to closely monitor and direct when and how the work got done. Indeed, the reorganization had left untouched procedural guidelines for everything from dealing with customers on the phone and steps in the billing process to how to run meetings to expectations of frequent inspections and continuous performance measurement.

When the CIAR team shared these findings with the unit leader, he took them to be "a negative report card," and at the first feedback presentation to the senior management team, the reaction was mixed. Some managers accepted the validity of the analysis; others did not. The group processed the feedback over the course of a six-hour meeting and decided on a limited experiment in one of the work groups: evaluating performance by task completion rather than number of hours put in. Another manifestation of the assumption of the need for control was the leaders' reluctance to share the Dual Agenda analysis with the unit as a whole. They were used to "cascading" decisions to group managers and then to frontline employees, and they were not particularly comfortable presenting problems to people and asking them to participate in finding solutions. Nevertheless, they agreed to the request of the CIAR team to do so, albeit in a limited way—the team got ninety minutes for feedback to the middle management group and thirty minutes for a presentation to the unit as a whole.

At the unitwide presentation, however, a surprising thing happened. Moved by the obvious excitement the feedback caused in the auditorium of 250 people, the unit leader spontaneously took the stage, put the key presentation slide back in the projector, and began to talk about the difficulty the managers had had in having outsiders tell them negative things about the way the organization was running. CIAR team members saw employees look at each other approvingly as he spoke candidly about these thoughts and reactions. He continued by saying that he wanted to change the culture: to introduce greater flexibility and with it greater responsibility—to empower people. And at that point he made the dramatic announcement, already alluded to in Chapter Three, that for a limited experimental time, all employees could participate in any of the flexible arrangements available by policy, as long as there was no interference with getting the work accomplished.

The event was a turning point for this organization. However, neither the hierarchical structure nor the culture of control suddenly disappeared. At first, managers retained their role in deciding on individual flexible schedule proposals, but fairly quickly the increasing complexity made it necessary for the groups to work out scheduling in a more coordinated way. This in effect started them on a gradual path toward greater empowerment and responsibility. Their improved performance helped ensure that the unit's experiment in flexibility would become standard practice at the end of the trial period, and eventually the work groups began participating in other decisions formerly the preserve of management, such as hiring and evaluation. When the time came for corporate empowerment training, many people in the unit judged their groups to be beyond what the training offered.

Conclusion

Although we have experienced success in helping work groups achieve small, concrete Dual Agenda "wins," diffusion of the CIAR process itself is more difficult. We have struggled in this effort for a number of reasons. First is the problem of allocating sufficient time to spend with the organization to oversee the process, particularly at its critical points, which are often impossible to anticipate. Second, we have found that it does not work to hand the effort over to internal change agents who have not themselves engaged in the process, but convincing organizations that engaging them is a necessary step is difficult. Third, instability in the organization and continuous restructuring make it difficult to sustain a change process, yet these are part of the reality inside many workplaces today. Last but not least, though ensuring senior management participation in the process is crucial, it is often hard to achieve.

Nonetheless, there have been instances in which the process did take hold. In these cases, the key factors were that the CIAR team successfully engaged a large part of the organization, particularly in the feedback and in active reflection about underlying assumptions and their effects; worked with an internal committee, particularly one with a committed champion; and stayed in touch with the organizations over a sufficient length of time for change to take hold.

Working with operational units is also key. Each work group needs to devise its own work practice changes. Experimental pilots may be helpful, but it is also possible by now that sufficient accumulated experience with this method exists to provide the "success" experience necessary to proceed without them in future Dual Agenda projects.

Finally, though the goal has always been systemic change in work practices, for those to be sustained requires also individual change, on both cognitive and noncognitive levels. This kind of individual involvement is necessary to make systemic change possible, for without personally experiencing the effects of gendered assumptions, serious consideration of alternatives will be extremely difficult. Only by bringing these personal experiences and their consequences to light—in a public forum where a shared understanding of the issues can emerge—will it be possible to consider alternatives to the practices that continuously reinforce gendered organizational norms. Unraveling the dynamic relationship between such individual change and the systemic changes that are the goal of Dual Agenda work is a future challenge in the development of CIAR.

CHAPTER 8

Looking Ahead to an Equitable World

When we think of an equitable world, we think of one in which women and men, of diverse racial and ethnic origins, from different social classes and geographical regions, healthy and disabled, of various ages, and of different sexual orientations, have equal access to opportunities and a fair distribution of constraints on their choices. A key component of such an equitable world is organizing different spheres of life—work, family, community—in such a way that people can succeed in the world of paid work and still care for one another and themselves. To achieve such a world requires changes on many levels: changes in policies and practices (at work, in the family, and in community organizations such as schools or hospitals), broad cultural change, and changes that allow individuals to develop their sense of self-esteem and self-worth from a variety of activities without regard to stereotypes. Women and men, no matter where and how they are positioned, could then freely move between different sectors of life and succeed in any. Men and women could relate to each other with respect for each other's worth without gender stereotyping or adversarial interaction.

Our work deals with one aspect of this broader vision—the workplace. A central message of this book is the need to embrace the diverse ways that people work and the different ways they want to relate to their work. To achieve this goal requires moving beyond current ideal-worker concepts; beyond the oversimplification of "family-friendly" laws, policies, and benefits; and beyond existing assumptions about men's and women's roles. Hence the need to focus on change in work practices and in the underlying assumptions, cultures, and structures that shape them.

Change at the level of work practices is difficult because it challenges the importance of work in people's lives. It requires dealing with mind-sets and feelings about commitment and competence that support established ways of working as well as the prominence of paid work in life. Such entrenched beliefs are particularly hard to deal with—even to talk about in work groups—because they touch on men's and women's sense of identity and self-esteem. We have tried to confront such assumptions and feelings in ourselves and our own work groups, and doing so has helped us better understand our organizational partners.

The change method we present, Collaborative Interactive Action Research (CIAR), offers a way to deal with these difficult issues. CIAR is effective because it provides both a conceptual framework and an intervention strategy for bringing to the surface, examining critically, and challenging underlying gendered assumptions about work and how it should be done and for dealing with the resistance that such a process is likely to produce. This combination led to the encouraging Dual Agenda results we report in this book. To conclude, we briefly review the central points conveyed in earlier chapters, directing readers' attention to how concepts and intervention strategy come together in CIAR.

Conceptual Framework and Intervention Strategy: The Essence of CIAR

This book describes a method, but integral to the method is a reconceptualization of the relationships among gender, paid work, and other parts of life. We have described the ways in which work organizations are masculine gendered and how they got to be that way. Understanding this phenomenon is crucial because it explains how workplaces reflect larger patterns in society that have evolved over a long period of time. Placing gender equity issues in this framework opens them up to examination without recrimination and creates the possibility for change.

Central to our conceptual understanding is the idea that the gendered segregation of spheres leads to gender inequities. In the workplace, perceived as a masculine sphere, a number of assumptions about work practices militate—often covertly— against women's being treated fairly. Thus the traditional image of the ideal worker as someone for whom work is primary and who demonstrates commitment by making personal sacrifices, doing whatever it takes to get the job done, spending a great deal of time on it, and being seen to do so, tends to undermine women, who still carry the main share of responsibility outside the formal workplace or who do not wish to sacrifice all for work. And it no longer fits many men who want to have a greater role in family and community or who want to participate in activities outside of paid employment.

The ideal worker image also embodies assumptions about competence that value stereotypically masculine ways of working—individualistically, competitively, hierarchically—and devalue or make invisible the relational skills that many women bring from the domestic sphere. Significantly, these formulations of commitment and competence also place constraints on men by creating the expectation that they will put their career ahead of all else and will employ masculine ways of working. The result of this gender segregation, therefore, is inequities in both spheres for both men and women.

The second key piece of our conceptual framework is the Dual Agenda. It derives from the finding that gendered workplaces have negative implications, not only for the people working in them who do not fit gendered norms but for organizational effectiveness as well. Thus changes that increase gender equity and benefit the lives of employees can also provide leverage for addressing key performance problems. What we have found is that when people, at any level in an organization, bring their personal concerns to a critical look at work practices, they tap great reserves of energy and creativity toward designing and implementing systemic and constructive change.

Joint Learning and Action

At the heart of CIAR is a strategy of joint learning and action based on the Dual Agenda. In general terms, action researchers from outside an organization work together with people inside to unearth gendered assumptions about how work is done; to understand how those assumptions affect people and performance, positively and negatively; and to envision and enact new ways of working that eliminate the negative impacts. To summarize from previous chapters, five interrelated aspects of CIAR support this learning-and-action agenda.

Intervention with Ideas

Every step that action researchers take in CIAR constitutes an intervention, and every intervention presents an opportunity for jointly reframing organizational issues from a Dual Agenda perspective. In the first conversations that initiate a project, stating both equity and effectiveness clearly as objectives is a critical step in opening up consideration of connections between them. Individual interviews likewise invite people to consider the connections between personal issues and performance issues, usually in ways they have not done before. Joint learning about how equity and effectiveness issues manifest themselves in the particular workplace builds through successive steps of individual interviews, group discussions, analysis, and formal feedback and discussion of the analysis and continues into the phase of action experiments and assessment of the resistance they invoke. A Dual Agenda analysis has the power to galvanize action because it emerges from this collective process of reinterpretation of organization members' experience through the researchers' lens of gender equity or work–personal life integration.

Working with Gendered Assumptions

Within the Dual Agenda framework, intervening with ideas necessarily involves bringing to light gendered assumptions. Working with these assumptions then moves beyond ideas to the level of feelings, in particular what it feels like to be committed and competent in a particular workplace. Many aspects of CIAR—for example, the practice of starting out with individual interviews, a context in which people feel relatively comfortable voicing true feelings and discussing "undiscussables"—derive from the need to acknowledge these feelings and to give people the opportunity to deal with them. Working at the level of underlying gendered assumptions is the most challenging aspect of Dual Agenda work, but it is also where the power to make significant changes in work practices really lies.

Interactive Collaboration and Inquiry

Another significant but more subtle point is the way in which each element of CIAR—interactive collaboration, research, and action—embodies a challenge to gendered organizational norms. CIAR action researchers intentionally disavow the expert role of outside consultants. They avoid one-sided diagnoses or prescriptions and instead try to stay in a mode of joint learning and cocreation through the entire process of data collection, analysis, and the search for solutions. Functioning effectively in this mode requires an attitude of mutual inquiry and an openness to having the expert role shift back and forth between outsiders and insiders, each of whom holds critical parts of the requisite knowledge and understanding—what we have called the principle of fluid expertise.

Working with Resistance

Though the experimental frame makes it possible for people to suspend assumptions sufficiently to try new ways of working, it also creates resistance. CIAR views resistance as an opportunity to learn more about underlying assumptions that hold the established ways of working in place. Engaging this resistance allows researchers and organization members alike to experience the feelings involved in altering patterns that relate to notions of competence, commitment, and individual identity. And because the CIAR change process is iterative and allows for continuing evaluation and midcourse corrections, engaging resistance in this way leads to deeper learning. Revealing and then addressing legitimate concerns at a site improves the change effort by creating models that are more likely to be sustained than if one merely imported ideas from other sites.

Working on Multiple Levels

Finally, for change to be lasting, new modes of thinking and action are necessary at three levels — individual, group, and system. Individuals need also to experience multilevel change, shifts in both cognitive and noncognitive understanding. Key elements of CIAR aim to get at these multiple levels. For example, the interplay between individual interviews and group discussions enables underlying assumptions and the feelings that go with them to emerge for sharing in a safe setting. At the system level, people have the experience of understanding the analysis the CIAR team presents in its feedback and then brainstorming and implementing changes in response. Through this experience, they come to appreciate the *process* of Dual Agenda change as well as the concrete results.

Looking Ahead: Challenges and Opportunities

In Chapter Seven, we discussed the challenges of diffusing Dual Agenda change within organizations, but it is important also to diffuse more broadly, across organizations and into the culture at large. The issue here relates to both supply and demand: *supply* of people who understand the CIAR concept and process of change and can carry the work forward and *demand* within organizations and society to have it done. Dual Agenda change is time-consuming and personally challenging. Finding the people willing and able to do it and creating the felt need to make such an effort worthwhile are critical challenges for the future.

On the supply side, disseminating the ideas and working with all kinds of change agents, in many different kinds of organizations, and in both the Western developed economies and developing countries, will not be easy. We hope that this book and other publications on the Dual Agenda will help spread these ideas. But as we have said, more than cognitive knowledge is at stake. Our research has shown that personally experiencing the process and the feelings that it evokes is an important underpinning for understanding. The Change Agent Project of the Center for Gender in Organizations at the Simmons Graduate School of Management can help encourage this understanding.

An even more difficult challenge is creating the demand for this approach. How can one generate sufficient "pull" from the workplace to spark really widespread change, on the scale, for example, of the total quality movement? In *The Time Bind*, Arlie Hochschild points to a paradox of the twenty-first-century workplace: despite widespread complaints of overwork, many people don't *want* more time at home. Many people, suggests Hochschild, find it tough to raise children and to be involved in community. They lack the skills for it and feel inadequate; they would rather be at work, where they know what it means to be competent.[1] In our own work in organizations, we have sometimes joked that we would have to give workshops on what to do with free time if people actually worked less. We had a sense that some people, especially men, would not know what to do with their time and would not have a strong desire to get into family or community work because that is seen as "women's work" and not valued in society. So one important challenge for large-scale diffusion is to create a broader demand for this kind of change.

Creating such demand will require a significant cultural shift. Indeed, it will require recasting engagement in family and community, not as a constraint to work success, but as a joyful, learning, satisfying activity that builds self-worth and the skills and abilities that make people full human beings, able to work and interact effectively with others and enjoy life. Such a transformation is likely to be a hard sell to men, as well as some women, who have not had the experience of this kind of growth through connection.

Nonetheless, hopeful signs are beginning to appear. One is evidence of growing recognition of the value of and need for relational competence in the workplace. Research on management, for example, as reported in *Business Week* in November 2000, has shown women consistently rating higher than men in peer performance evaluations of capabilities such as motivating others, fostering communication, and producing high-quality work. As Rosabeth Moss Kanter noted, these are "exactly those skills needed to succeed in the global Information Age." Interviewees for this article also gave women high marks for being less individualistic—less concerned with personal achievement and more so with overall success.[2] And a recent analysis of several data sets shows that "women are more likely than men to disapprove of the practice of accepting bribes," that "firms owned or managed by women are less likely to be involved in bribe-giving," and that "higher levels of women's participation in public life are associated with lower levels of corruption."[3] Such results may well increase the demand for relational competence and with it the realization that it can be best learned in the private sphere of family and community activities.

To the extent that the revaluing of relational skills in the workplace supports men who want to devote more time outside it, there is need for a parallel opening up of family structures and cultures to make a place for them. In Philadelphia, the Third Path Institute under Jessica DeGroot is working with parent couples on what they call "shared care." "Shared Care parents work while continuing to create time for the important job of caring for family. Both 'family' and 'work' are redesigned to allow parents equal access to success at work and success at home. . . . Shared Care parents redesign work around the needs of family, change solutions as the needs of children change, maximize the use of parental care and extended family, [and] create a shared involvement of caring for children and earning income."[4]

By developing workshops for young couples to support them in making conscious choices about how to manage careers and family, DeGroot and her colleagues allow couples to dream and envision a life different from what their parents had. This may seem a small step, perhaps, but its wide reception in the media indicates that demand for change in the direction of our work may be growing.[5]

Conclusion: The Equity Imperative Revisited

Our final point goes back to the effects of globalization. The internationalization of the economy is spreading the assumptions and norms of developed countries—about ways of working and about the place of work in people's lives throughout the world.

We see this trend as potentially dangerous because of the negative consequences of the Western pattern of the relationship to work for other spheres of life, particularly for families and communities. There are several key elements in this pattern: the segregation of personal and family life from work life, with work being given priority in ways that increase the conflict between work and the rest of life; an emphasis on individual achievement and material success; and the assumption that to achieve, individuals and work organizations need to be highly competitive.

This pattern is costly in that it is associated with serious problems for society, among them marital and family problems, concerns about what is happening to the next generation, problems with elder care, community problems, and health problems. Yet we continue to export our ingrained assumptions and beliefs that this is the "best" way to operate to countries with different cultures, values, and structures. As noted in Chapter Two, the current Western pattern emerged relatively recently and does not exist everywhere. But Westerners tend to regard other patterns as inferior.

Not all Western industrialized societies have responded in the same way or at the same pace to the problems these patterns cause. In Chapter One, we mentioned legislative initiatives in Britain, the Netherlands, and France. And the Scandinavian experience is significant. In Sweden, parental leaves for both men and women have been part of a twenty-five-year legislative agenda to promote gender equity and support male parenting. In Norway, a 1995 law, patterned on one in Sweden, established a "daddy's month" of parental leave, which families lose if fathers don't use it. Within two years, 80 percent of Norwegian fathers were using the leave. Women in Norway and Sweden still carry the main burden of family responsibilities, but these are noteworthy changes. Perhaps most significant, they represent a societywide consensus about the importance of children and the important role both parents have in child care.[6]

Despite the crisis of care, we are still a long way from such a consensus in the United States. And despite the problems that our established ways of working cause, we are only just beginning to look at the possibility that we do not have to work the way we do or give work the primacy it has in order to compete successfully. But it is urgent that we reconsider our exporting of nonfamily, noncommunity values to "less developed" societies and worry about the inequities that may result. This equity imperative, which argues for taking up the Dual Agenda on a broad scale—including consideration of racial, ethnic, and other inequities—has motivated the work reported in this book.

Appendix:
The Book in Context

Bettye H. Pruitt

The purpose of this appendix is to place the findings and analysis presented in this book in longer-term perspective and a larger context in order to clarify their significance and enhance their usefulness. The task of pulling together this story has fallen to me, the historian in the group. When I joined the book-writing effort, the plan was for twelve coauthors to produce topical chapters in teams, coming together to discuss issues as a single group in one or more working retreats. My role was to provide, in a historical overview of the emergence of the Dual Agenda and Collaborative Interactive Action Research (CIAR), a framework that would help readers see and interpret the individual chapters as part of an integrated, though multifaceted, body of ideas and experience. Eventually it became obvious that too many of the coauthors for one reason or another found this project design unworkable. Rhona Rapoport, Lotte Bailyn, and Joyce Fletcher then invited me to join them in writing a different kind of book—one that is, as we state in the Preface, both more fully integrated and synthesized and less rich in variety of subject matter, viewpoint, and emphasis.

Connection and continuity are less essential to this kind of book, and the story it tells is neither as detailed nor as broad in scope as originally planned. Yet we still think it is important to connect ideas and arguments to the human beings behind them by describing some of the ways in which personal circumstances, interests, concerns, and interactions have influenced and continue to influence their evolution. This goal is in keeping with our emphasis on bringing personal stories and issues into workplace conversations. It also reflects our desire to convey the work-in-progress nature of CIAR and so to be inviting of others who might consider taking it up and developing it further. Finally, we hope that telling this story will be another way of acknowledging the contributions of the many people who have played important roles in advancing the Dual Agenda concept and CIAR and who continue to do so.

Conceptual Origins of a Different Approach to Work and Family

As we have described, the inspiration for this book came out of the Ford Foundation–funded Xerox project of the early 1990s. Yet as in most undertakings, it has roots in the prior work and experience of the authors. For Rhona Rapoport, these connections reach back into her childhood in South Africa, where she developed an abiding interest in equity issues. In the 1950s, her doctoral dissertation in sociology for the London School of Economics was a study of the impact of industrialization on families in Uganda. In the 1960s, having completed a postdoctoral training program in psychoanalysis, she and her husband, the anthropologist Robert N. Rapoport, began joint studies of work-family issues. She had been examining critical transition points in families, such as marriage and having a first baby, and he had been looking at the career transitions of professionals. Together they recognized the significance of the interaction between these events in work and family.

The Rapoports started a study of engineering students who were about to get married, following them through that transition and into their early careers. This was before "work-family" was an established field of research in any academic discipline. Instead, the Rapoports noted, work and family were segregated conceptually, paralleling the practical and social separation that had occurred when, with the coming of the Industrial Revolution, families stopped functioning as units of economic production.[1]

They sustained their interest in this subject and in 1971 produced a major study of British professional couples with children: *Dual-Career Families.* A significant aspect of this work was that it looked at the challenges involved in combining career and family in structural terms, rather than in terms of problems and dilemmas to be resolved individually, in particular by individual women. The Rapoports gave equal attention to both men and women in dual-career couples, and they examined the interaction of individual choices, attitudes, and feelings with broader social factors. For example, in looking at work overload as a source of stress, they considered both the specific practical problems involved and the context of social and personal norms around men's and women's roles in the family, within which people were wrestling with those problems.[2]

In 1973, in London, the Rapoports formed the Institute for Family and Environmental Research, providing a home for continuing research in the work-family field. As the field evolved, and as the dual-career family pattern became more common and accepted, public attention shifted toward the workplace as the source of difficulties for people to manage both work and personal life. The emergence of family-friendly policies, in the 1980s, is largely attributable to this shift. As the Rapoports also gave greater attention to the work side of work and family, they began focusing on the workplace norms that undermine women at work and men at home—for example, rigid expectations about where and when work must be done, conventional ideas about how work should be conducted, and a pervasive work ethic "that has an insatiability attached to it, particularly in relation to males."[3]

By the late 1980s, Rhona Rapoport's research and writing in particular were focused on these workplace issues, which seemed increasingly relevant as policymakers began to face the disappointing results of family-friendly workplace initiatives.[4] Her conceptual understanding made a good fit with the interests of June Zeitlin at the Ford Foundation, which had supported the development of these initiatives with its funding programs. Rapoport also contributed methodological understanding about how to conduct research on complicated and often tacit social norms—just the kind of research that seemed to be needed to approach work-family issues in a new way. In their studies of couples, the Rapoports had developed a method they called Collaborative Interviewing and Interactive Research. Both her psychoanalytic training and their joint association with the Tavistock Institute of Human Relations, a leading institution in the development of action research, informed this approach. It involved conducting interviews as two-way conversations in which both parties participated in uncovering and making sense of the interviewee's experience. Thus the research "subjects" became actively engaged in the research and learning enterprise—a central methodological principle carried over into the proposal Zeitlin and Rapoport made to corporations in their search for research partners.[5]

When they considered whom they wanted to recruit to conduct this research, Lotte Bailyn, a professor at MIT's Sloan School of Management, was a natural choice. Bailyn's longtime research interest focused on professional careers. She had first written about the difference in the choices available to professional men and women in the early 1960s,[6] joining the Rapoports in the tiny community of scholars looking at the intersection between work and family issues.[7] A few years later, Bailyn collaborated on the analysis of questionnaire data the Rapoports had collected from women university graduates and their partners, looking at the factors that made for a more or less satisfactory arrangement for these couples.[8]

Pursuing this line of inquiry, she had reached the conclusion by the mid-1980s that the way work itself is organized—around stereotypical male employees with no significant responsibilities outside of the workplace—is often the major obstacle for people trying to combine work and family.[9] And she had begun to make the connection between equity and effectiveness that is the foundation for the Dual Agenda. For example, in a study published in 1989, comparing two groups of systems developers, one home-based and one office-based, Bailyn found significant advantages for work effectiveness in the home-based setting—for instance, a view of personal success focused on performing assigned tasks well, rather than on advancement in the organizational hierarchy.[10] In *Breaking the Mold*, she went a step further, providing an early statement of the equity imperative. "These are not peripheral issues," Bailyn wrote. "On the contrary, they lie at the core of the challenges facing American industry. . . . Companies must include—explicitly, imaginatively, and effectively—the private needs of employees when reengineering their work. Only if they do so can they gain a competitive edge."[11] In short, Bailyn offered just the kind of fresh perspective that Zeitlin and Rapoport were seeking for the new research initiative.

From Ideas to Action Research: The Xerox Project Team

Ultimately, as we have described, three companies signed on to do this research: Xerox Corporation; Corning, Inc.; and Tandem Computers. Between 1990 and 1996, three multiyear projects started up sequentially (at Corning in 1990, at Xerox in 1991, and at Tandem in 1993), each with a separate research team and a distinctive approach. Rhona Rapoport provided coordination to the overall research initiative and an "inside outsider" view to all three of the teams.[12]

At Corning, a team of work-family experts from the Families and Work Institute (FWI), including Ellen Galinsky, Dana Friedman, and James Levine, linked its research to an ongoing Corning initiative on workforce diversity.[13] The research team at Tandem came from an organizational development firm, Artemis Management Consultants, led by Barbara Miller. This team emphasized interpersonal relationships and individual change as well as institutional change.[14] At Xerox, a team of academic researchers co-led by Lotte Bailyn focused on testing the hypothesis that had emerged from Bailyn's research, "that it is possible to use work-family issues as a lever for change that enhances productivity, ensures gender equity, and eases the conflict between work and family."[15]

To codirect the Xerox project, Bailyn recruited Deborah M. Kolb, then associate executive director of the Harvard Program on Negotiation and a professor at the Simmons Graduate School of Management. Kolb had built her academic career on the study of mediation and conflict resolution, but only recently had she begun looking at gender issues in that field. "When I got to the program on negotiation," she recalled, "I became an instant expert on gender. They used to ask me to come to a class and talk about gender negotiations because I was the only woman. I was the only one who had gender, right? So I got interested in gender." Though not professionally interested in work-family issues, Kolb saw an opportunity to deepen her understanding of gender issues in the workplace through the Xerox study and to contribute to it from her background in negotiation. From that background, she helped establish a key element of the research stance in Dual Agenda, the notion that the action researchers bring an organizational change agenda (equity) that exists independently from the organization's agenda and that there may or may not be a fit between the two.[16]

Bailyn and Kolb rounded out the academic contingent of the Xerox research team with three doctoral students, Leslie Perlow, Robin Johnson, and Joyce K. Fletcher, and somewhat later in the project added Susan Eaton, who was in transition from a career in the labor movement to doctoral studies. Maureen Harvey, an

organizational development professional, brought the analytical and methodological skills of an experienced interventionist.
Inevitably, each team member's personal interests and conceptual perspectives helped shape the research and contributed to
its results. The ability of the student-researchers to spend substantial amounts of time on-site was a significant aspect of this
project, and all three doctoral candidates produced dissertations
from their Xerox work. Perlow became particularly interested in
examining the assumption that work performance relates directly to the amount of time spent on work—an interest carried into
her intensive study of the quiet-time experiment and to other
aspects of the use of time in the workplace.[17] Johnson's dissertation research focused on empowerment.[18] She came to the Xerox
project as an experienced manager and was the only woman of
color on the research team. Her concern for how social identity
characteristics such as race and class intersect with gender issues
did not become a major theme in the Xerox work but influenced
it and helped prepare the way for subsequent investigations, most
notably ongoing work at the Center for Gender in Organizations,
as described later in the section "Expanding the Network: Focus
on Gender Equity."

All of these team members contributed significantly to the
results of the Xerox project and, through their participation on
the action research team, to the methodological understanding that came out of it. As far as this book is concerned, however,
two Xerox team members, Fletcher and Harvey, played a particularly important role. They brought with them into the project a stream of thought that forms a key strand of both the
concepts and method presented here—the feminist theory of relational practice.

Deborah Kolb got the idea of inviting Joyce Fletcher to join
the Xerox team while giving a workshop on negotiation. Fletcher,

then pursuing a doctoral degree in management, asked an intriguing question from the audience, in which she framed what Kolb had been talking about as "invisible work." This framing reflected a deep interest in understanding how the skills and values associated with the nurturing role women are acculturated to play in the domestic sphere carry over into the workplace and how women fare in that setting. Fletcher had initially been inspired to consider these questions by the groundbreaking work of the feminist psychologist Jean Baker Miller. Miller's *Toward a New Psychology of Women* (1976), she recalled, had first given her the idea "that the relational traits I valued in myself and others, such as empathy, vulnerability, and connection, could be conceptualized as strengths rather than weaknesses or emotional dependencies." At the same time, Miller had suggested that the way men are socialized, "to devalue and deny in themselves [those same] relational skills," contributed to the devaluing of relational work in society as a whole. Fletcher's research interest was in using these feminist insights to understand the essential but largely invisible role of relational skills in the workplace.[19]

On impulse, at the end of their conversation, Kolb invited Fletcher to join the Xerox research team, and though she was not professionally interested in work-family issues, she accepted. The feminist thinking she brought into the Xerox team made other team members uncomfortable at first, but (in keeping with relational theory) through a process of mutual influence, these ideas eventually became fully interwoven with the analysis of organizational norms emerging in the work-family field. In fact, in examining the role of relational skills in the workplace, Fletcher was mirroring a strand of inquiry from the Rapoports' 1975 essay, "Men, Women, and Equity," in which they wrote: "When women are introduced into the workplace and manifest traits that many men have suppressed, tension may increase. In addition, these modes of behavior seem to tradition-minded men as alien to the workplace. On the other hand, whether or not women are more emotional and expressive than men, and whether or not this is something linked to their biology or to a particular culture and historical phase, there is now a basis for redefining this kind of characteristic as adaptive in certain modern situations."[20]

Maureen Harvey also brought relational theory into the team, from a practical rather than a theoretical understanding. She came to the Xerox project with more than twenty years' experience as an internal organizational development consultant for Digital Equipment Corporation (DEC). In the 1980s, she had focused increasingly on diversity issues, including the challenges of bringing women up through the ranks to positions of leadership; and in 1991, she had orchestrated a project with the Stone Center of Wellesley College, which brought Jean Baker Miller into DEC to help work on gender issues. This work had brought her into contact with Fletcher, and Harvey's presentation at the Stone Center on this project caught the attention of Bailyn and Fletcher and prompted them to invite her to join the Xerox project. In that and subsequent Dual Agenda projects, Harvey taught by example, as well as through extensive written communication and conversation, what it means to put relational skills into practice in work settings.[21]

The combination of an interventionist's skills and perspective with those of academic researchers was an important factor in enabling the research team to move successfully into and through the action experiments of the Xerox project. Another key factor was the participation of the Xerox members of the Collaborative Action Research Team (CART), the main contact group in the corporation: Anne Mulcahy, Patricia Nazemetz, Wendy Starr,

Carole Cornall, Ruth Fattori, Don Zrebiec, Sheila Collier, and Janet Gill Hernandez. This group met with Zeitlin, Rapoport, Bailyn, and Kolb at the very beginning to frame the project. They helped cast it in a way that would be effective in Xerox's organizational culture, using the quality model. Subsequently, they played a key role on a continuing basis, particularly in helping to set the criteria for site selection and then identifying sites to do the work. This group and all the individuals in the units who participated in the research made it possible to enact the original design concept for the project of conducting action research in full partnership with the organization. As the project proceeded, Xerox became a funding partner as well.[22]

The research team worked intensively with three sites, all quite different organizations in terms of function, personnel, and business issues. All faced serious issues of work–personal life conflict, despite Xerox's well-established formal policies for leaves and flexible work arrangements. The action research initiative focused on understanding what was keeping people from using those benefits and on defining and trying out work practice changes that would remove those barriers. As the results of the action research came in, the research team began an intensive process of analyzing and reporting on the learning coming out of this effort. The concept of the Dual Agenda emerged from this process.[23]

Xerox Project Outcome: "Unexpected Connections"

The implications of the Xerox project findings amount, in June Zeitlin's words, to a "paradigm shift" for work organizations, from a worldview in which work and personal-life concerns are separate and in competition to one in which they can be integrated synergistically. The findings challenge organizational leaders to take a more systemic and strategic approach in dealing with employees' work and personal-life issues. But, Zeitlin has suggested, they also challenge those individuals who wish to pursue both paid work and personal-life commitments, without painful sacrifices in either, to assert their right to do so. Said Zeitlin, "This is where women and men together must use their collective power to truly transform the workplace."[24]

In terms of scale and significance, such a shift would be comparable to the mind-set change involved in the total quality management (TQM) revolution of the 1980s. In fact, Lotte Bailyn recalls, it was a corporate executive participating in a leadership conference discussion group about the Xerox research and the Dual Agenda who first made this comparison. Adopting TQM, he pointed out, involved manufacturers' letting go of the received wisdom that product quality and low-cost production were mutually exclusive choices and opening up to the possibility that with the adoption of different manufacturing practices, they could become mutually reinforcing instead. Of course, in the case of quality, the example and competitive challenge presented by Japan to the rest of the industrialized world helped drive this mind-set change. From the perspective of corporate top management, the set of crisis conditions that might compel rapid change in the area of gender equity and work–personal life integration—the equity imperative—is more amorphous and less clearly definable as a pressing business problem. So what we see in this case is a process of gradual expansion of familiarity with and openness to the Dual Agenda concept as more people become engaged in working with it and writing about it.

Expanding the Network: Focus on Work–Personal Life Integration

A critical transition, which this book aims to further, is the movement of both the Dual Agenda concept and the CIAR method beyond the academic realm, in which they first emerged and where they continue to develop, into wider practical application as well as into the public discourse on equity and work–personal life issues. Since the appearance in November 1996 of the formal report to the Ford Foundation on the Xerox-Tandem-Corning research initiative, titled *Relinking Life and Work: Toward a Better Future,* members of all three research teams have contributed to this transition. Although the *Relinking* report focuses primarily on the Xerox project and findings, the Corning and Tandem research teams participated in the analysis and report writing, and much of the methodological understanding presented in this book reflects shared learning from those related but quite different project experiences. And they continue to explore the issues defined in the *Relinking* report in the context of their ongoing work.

Continuing a stream of research begun in the 1980s, nationally representative studies conducted by FWI in 1997 and 2001 link quality of life at work to employees' commitment, job satisfaction, loyalty, and well-being. In *Ask the Children,* the first comprehensive study of work-family issues to include both children and parents, FWI president Ellen Galinsky challenges the concept of balance and the either-or dichotomy it implies. Galinsky has carried these research findings to a wide public audience, as a frequent talk show guest on U.S. network television and as a featured speaker at meetings on work-family and work-life issues in the United States and internationally. Similarly, the long-running Fatherhood Project, conducted by James Levine, has drawn attention to aspects of workplaces that are not "father-friendly."[25] And Dana Friedman, cofounder with Ellen Galinsky of FWI, continues to further this perspective, now in her current role as senior vice president at Bright Horizons Family Solutions, Inc.

Barbara Miller has also incorporated the Dual Agenda concept and language into the ongoing work of Artemis Management Consultants. In a 2000 publication, she describes developing and piloting with Hewlett Packard/Agilent Technologies a workbook, *Reinventing Work: Innovative Strategies Relinking Life and Livelihood to Benefit Business and Staff,* building on the learning from the Xerox project and her related research at Tandem Computers. Miller's approach blends the Dual Agenda and a methodological focus on the assumptions underlying work practices with what she calls "traditional work redesign tools" aimed at improving "three bottom lines in organizations: profitability or shareholder value, customer satisfaction, and employee satisfaction." She describes beneficial work practice changes that have resulted from this approach as well as the continuing development of her change method.[26]

The network of people using the Dual Agenda concept in their work has also expanded through additional action research projects. In 1995, work-family issues became part of discussions among fifty national leaders attending the opening conference of the New Economic Equation project at the Radcliffe Public Policy Center (RPPC). One of the conference participants was Terrance Murray, chairman and CEO of Fleet Financial Group. As part of Fleet's contribution to the New Economic Equation project, Murray set in motion the steps leading to a Dual

Agenda project at Fleet, with Lotte Bailyn and Paula Rayman, RPPC's director, as principal investigators.[27] In Jill Casner-Lotto's *Holding a Job, Having a Life: Strategies for Change* (2000), the Work in America Institute included the Radcliffe-Fleet project in its report on efforts in the U.S. corporate world to move beyond policy solutions to work–personal life issues. This report, funded by the Ford Foundation, includes five cases of work practice changes of the kind we discuss in this book. Seven other cases describe cultural change and other initiatives, which Casner-Lotto also defines as "designed to accomplish a 'dual agenda': to simultaneously improve business results and employees' work/life integration."[28]

The inclusion of Dual Agenda issues and language in the conferences and publications of long-established public policy and business policy research institutes such as RPPC and the Work in America Institute is an important step in helping to move the discussion of and action on work–personal life integration into a broader forum. Another promising development of this sort is the creation in 2001 at the Sloan School of Management of the MIT Workplace Center. This center is to be directed jointly by Lotte Bailyn and Thomas Kochan and funded by the Alfred P. Sloan Foundation. The center is dedicated to expanding the research on the work-family relationship to all levels of work, from manual and clerical labor to executive and professional offices, and to encompass the study of how institutions outside the workplace (community institutions, labor unions, government) shape work-family interactions. Significantly, the center's mission also has a major component of intervention, as well as public education and stakeholder dialogues about work-family issues. The Dual Agenda and CIAR are incorporated into its approach, but by encompassing a larger institutional context, the center aims to continue the development of methods and understandings beyond what is reflected in this book.[29]

In addition to these U.S.-centered developments, the *Relinking Life and Work* report and the Dual Agenda concept have forged a connection with people engaged in work-family change initiatives and research in Europe. In Norway, Ragnhild Sohlberg, vice president of corporate staff at Norsk Hydro ASA, and others have been actively involved in changes in her company and in the country at large, aimed at making workplaces more friendly to working families and at the same time improving effectiveness in the workplace. Louise Boelens, an organizational consultant based in Utrecht, Netherlands, is conducting a "relinking study" with the faculty of a large school in Amsterdam, a project funded in part by the Dutch government. In the United Kingdom, Shirley Dex of the Judge Institute for Management Studies at Cambridge University has been working with a U.K.-based multinational technology firm to institute changes that will help employees ease work–personal life conflicts while also allowing the company to maintain its productivity. Suzan Lewis, professor of organizational and work-life psychology at Manchester Metropolitan University, serves as a consultant to organizations in the United Kingdom, including a government department, injecting into work-life balance initiatives the idea of the Dual Agenda and a sense of the importance of focusing on systemic as well as individual change. These activities are a hopeful sign that the timing is favorable for our vision of work–personal life integration to spread broadly on an international basis.[30]

Expanding the Network: Focus on Gender Equity

At the same time, since the Xerox project, there have been a number of Dual Agenda initiatives aimed more explicitly at advancing gender equity and linked by the common threads of Ford Foundation funding and the participation of Rhona Rapoport as the "inside outsider" consultant to the project teams. As in the work-family area, these initiatives have brought in others who have continued the dissemination and development of the concept and the CIAR method even as they have adapted it to their own interests and concerns. One was a project with The Body Shop, launched in 1995 and led by Debra Meyerson and Deborah Kolb and involving Robin Ely, Gill Coleman, Ann Rippin, and Maureen Harvey. This project produced a valuable analytical framework for understanding issues of gender equity[31] and a number of methodological insights—for example, about the importance of changing how people talk and think about organizational realities.[32] In addition, through Coleman and Rippin, it widened the network of people working on the Dual Agenda in the United Kingdom. For example, Coleman, who is director of the New Academy of Business in Bristol, England, is supporting a Dual Agenda initiative in a UK government department, initiated by a graduate of the academy's management science program.[33]

In addition, in 1992 and 1996, the Ford Foundation funded projects in member organizations of the Consultative Group on International Agricultural Research (CGIAR), a global consortium of sixteen research centers, involving Deborah Merrill-Sands as project leader. Trained as an anthropologist, Merrill-Sands had been a longtime CGIAR employee, working first as a researcher and research manager and subsequently as leader of an internal CGIAR study on gender issues affecting scientific staff. She learned of the Xerox work through the Ford Foundation and brought in Kolb and Fletcher, among others, as coinvestigators in the CGIAR projects. Those projects produced significant learning about CIAR, in particular about the role of cultural analysis and the power of narratives coming out of it to create a supportive context for work practice changes.[34]

Many of these individual strands came together with the creation of the Center for Gender in Organizations (CGO) at the Simmons Graduate School of Management in Boston — again with Ford Foundation support. CGO originated in 1994 under Deborah Kolb's direction as the Gender and Organizational Change program of the Simmons Institute for Leadership and Change. In 1998, it became a separate center within the Simmons Graduate School of Management, with a mission of "advancing learning and understanding of the connection between gender, in all its complexities, and organizational effectiveness" and an objective of "working at the intersection of scholarship and practice."[35] This organization brought together many people with experience in Dual Agenda projects, including Kolb and Merrill-Sands as codirectors, Fletcher, Meyerson, Ely, and Coleman as faculty, and Rapoport as Distinguished Fellow. June Zeitlin, who left the Ford Foundation in 1999 to become executive director of the Women's Environment and Development Organization, and Jan Jaffe, who managed the Ford Foundation grants on Dual Agenda work after Zeitlin's departure, both participate in CGO conferences. At the same time, CGO is further widening the network of people working under the Dual Agenda umbrella, making it more international and diverse.[36]

With this greater human diversity has come greater diversity in thinking about CIAR as a way of producing Dual Agenda change. For example, CGO's initiatives toward building the capacity inside organizations to advance gender equity has been influenced by the long-term interest of CGO faculty Debra Meyerson and Maureen Scully in the role of change agents.[37] Joyce Fletcher has continued to pursue her concern with the role of relational practice in the workplace: in 1999, she wrote a CGO working paper on this topic with Roy Jacques, a member of the Artemis research team at Tandem Corporation; and she has maintained a connection to the Stone Center of Wellesley College as a researcher and a faculty member of the Jean Baker Miller Training Institute.[38]

In addition, as the CGO group has become larger and more diverse, diversity itself has become a more central and pressing issue. A feature of CGO is an annual conference bringing together academics and organizational practitioners for discussion of equity issues. The discussion in the 1998 conference began to challenge the understanding of gender as too narrow, privileging a dominant group of women. Out of that discussion came the theme for the 1999 conference: "Gender at Work: Beyond White, Western, Middle-Class, Heterosexual, Professional Women." As an outcome of this conference, a focus of CGO convening in 2000–2001 became "Building Alliances Across Differences as a Strategy for Organizational Change."[39]

Meanwhile, at MIT, Lotte Bailyn was also pursuing the gender equity thread, but in a different way. As chair of the MIT faculty, Bailyn oversaw the 1999 publication of *A Study on the Status of Women Faculty in Science at MIT.*[40] This report cannot really be considered Dual Agenda work but is related to it in that it is a powerful statement of the need for examining the ways in which university cultures and practices undermine the ability of senior women faculty to perform up to their full potential. The MIT report has received wide attention, both in the press and in the administrations of other leading U.S. universities, and its findings are echoed in statements by the new Princeton University president, Shirley Tilghman, questioning tenure as a system that is "no friend to women."[41] These developments are significant in themselves, of course. But they are also highly relevant to CIAR in that they address the kind of academic norms—for example, the singular emphasis on individual expertise in promotion and tenure decisions—that, as we have suggested in this book, contribute to the difficulty of achieving workplace equity.

Conclusion: Dual Agenda Thinking in the Ethos

Paralleling the creation of CGO in 1996, Xerox project colleagues Bailyn, Rapoport, Kolb, and Fletcher formed LUME International, LLP, to collaborate on Dual Agenda interventions specifically aimed at work–personal life issues. With Maureen Harvey, who became managing partner of LUME, they conducted several projects on a consulting basis, all of which contributed important learning about the CIAR method, as well as case material for this book.[42] One of the significant methodological questions LUME raised but did not answer before the group disbanded in 1999 was whether it is possible to replicate the Xerox project results if the action researchers come in as consultants, without the independent status of academic researchers and without at least partial outside funding, such as that from the Ford Foundation. In the 1990s, corporate commitment to the difficult work CIAR entails remained extremely fragile in the face of challenges such as budget cuts, downsizings, restructurings, and the increasingly frenetic pace of business life.

Yet in the same period, Dual Agenda topics have become part of leadership conferences, like the one at RPPC. Articles in the *MIT Sloan Management Review* and *Harvard Business Review*[43] have introduced key concepts and findings into the mainstream of business thinking, and similarly, the activities of the Families and Work Institute have carried them into public discourse on work-family issues. And action research initiatives continue. Placing these recent developments in the context of the long-term gestation of the ideas offers some encouragement about the ultimate outcome. The challenges remain great, but at least the ideas and the environment seem to be evolving together, and we can hope that broad cultural change on these issues may provide a positive context in which individuals and groups may be more inclined to take up June Zeitlin's challenge to assert their right to a workplace that permits work–personal life integration. Getting these ideas about gender equity and work–personal life integration into the ethos is an important goal of this book, but not the only one by any means. Doing so in a method book is aimed at conveying the message that change is possible, though difficult.

Looking at all the diversity of thinking, concern, and interest Dual Agenda research is generating, it is not surprising that a group of twelve would find it difficult to undertake the task of jointly producing a book on method. The objection that there were too many unanswered questions and unresolved disagreements about how best to advance the Dual Agenda in organizations make a lot of sense in this context. To cite just one example, there is debate over whether, from a tactical perspective, gender equity or work–personal life integration makes a better entering focus for Dual Agenda interventions. It is with these issues in mind that we have emphasized that CIAR is still emerging as a method, still "under development."

One may well ask, why produce a method book if the method is not fully worked out? The answer in this case is that the method, like the Dual Agenda concept, needs to move out of the academic, "experimental" realm. The central hypothesis that Dual Agenda change is possible has been proved. The research now needs to focus on how to make that change more robust and how to make it more widespread. To accomplish this task, many more people need to try it, work with the CIAR method, build on it, and improve it. To the extent that this book contributes to that necessary development, it will have served the purpose of its authors.

Notes

Preface

1. June Zeitlin, "Preface," in Rhona Rapoport and others, *Relinking Life and Work: Toward a Better Future* (New York: Ford Foundation, 1996), p. 3.

2. Zeitlin, "Preface," pp. 3–4. See also Lotte Bailyn, Joyce K. Fletcher, and Deborah M. Kolb, "Unexpected Connections: Considering Employees' Personal Lives Can Revitalize Your Business," *Sloan Management Review,* 1997, 38(4), 11–19.

Chapter One

1. We thank Ragnhild Sohlberg for sharing this perspective on the global dynamic. Ragnhild Sohlberg, personal communication, Aug. 8, 2001.

2. These particular statements were made in relation to a high-profile legal suit against Ernst & Young; see Jeffrey Krasner, "Hitting the Glass Ceiling," *Boston Sunday Globe,* May 30, 2001, p. G1.

3. Center for Policy Alternatives and Lifetime Television, "Women's Voices, 2000: The Most Comprehensive Polling and Research Project on Women's Values and Policy Priorities for the Economy," http://www.stateaction.org, 2000.

4. See National Sleep Foundation, "Sleep in America, 2001," http://www.sleepfoundation.org/publications/2001poll.html, Mar. 2001.

5. Mona Harrington, *Care and Equality: Inventing a New Family Politics* (New York: Knopf, 1999), pp. 152–153.

6. Joan Williams, *Unbending Gender: Why Family and Work Conflict and What to Do About It* (New York: Oxford University Press, 2000).

7. James A. Levine and Todd L. Pittinsky, *Working Fathers: New Strategies for Balancing Work and Family* (Reading, Mass.: Addison-Wesley, 1997).

8. Richard Carelli, "Work Isn't All, Rehnquist Tells Law School Graduates," *Boston Globe*, May 29, 2000, p. A10.

9. Robert B. Reich, *The Future of Success* (New York: Knopf, 2001).

10. Joe Sharkey, "The World Bank Gauges the Toll Travel Takes on Employees and Looks for Ways to Soften the Effect," *New York Times*, May 10, 2000, p. M1.

11. Elizabeth Thomson, "The Cost of Depression," *MIT Tech Talk*, Aug. 23, 2000, p. 3.

12. Ellen Galinsky, Stacy S. Kim, and James T. Bond, *Feeling Overworked: When Work Becomes Too Much* (Scarsdale, N.Y.: Families and Work Institute, 2001).

13. Charles Fishman, "Sanity, Inc.," *Fast Company*, Jan. 1999, pp. 84–96.

14. Marian Ruderman, and Patricia Ohlott, *Standing at the Crossroads: Next Steps for Developing High-Achieving Women* (San Francisco: Jossey-Bass, 2002).

15. See, for example, Richard L. Berke, "Bush Is Providing Corporate Model for White House," *New York Times on the Web*, Mar. 11, 2001.

16. United Nations Development Programme, "The Invisible Heart: Care and the Global Economy," in *Human Development Report, 1999* (New York: Oxford University Press, 1999).

17. For a similar approach challenging masculine gendered norms, in this case in the field of economics, see Julie A. Nelson, "The Study of Choice or the Study of Provisioning? Gender and the Definition of Economics," in Marianne A. Ferber and Julie A. Nelson (eds.), *Beyond Economic Man: Feminist Theory and Economics* (Chicago: University of Chicago Press, 1993).

18. Arlie Hochschild, *The Second Shift: Working Parents and the Revolution at Home* (New York: Viking, 1989); Lotte Bailyn, *Breaking the Mold: Women, Men, and Time in the New Corporate World* (New York: Free Press, 1993). Rhona and Robert Rapoport emphasize the necessity of distinguishing between equality of opportunity and equality of conditions; Rhona Rapoport and Robert N. Rapoport, "Men, Women, and Equity," *Family Coordinator*, Oct. 1975, pp. 421–432.

19. Rhona Rapoport and Robert N. Rapoport, *Dual-Career Families* (Harmondsworth, England: Penguin, 1971).

20. See Alice S. Rossi, "Equality Between the Sexes: An Immodest Proposal," *Daedalus*, 1964, 93, 638–646; Lotte Bailyn, "Notes on the Role of Choice in the Psychology of Professional Women," *Daedalus*, 1964, 93, 700–710; and Edmund Dahlström and Rita Liljeström, *The Changing Roles of Men and Women* (London: Duckworth, 1967).

21. Rosabeth Moss Kanter, *Work and Family in the United States: A Critical Review and Agenda for Research and Policy* (New York: Russell Sage Foundation, 1977); Rosabeth Moss Kanter, *Men and Women of the Corporation* (New York: Basic Books, 1977); Hochschild, *The Second Shift*; Juliet Schor, *The Overworked American: The Unexpected Decline of Leisure* (New York: Basic Books, 1991); Bailyn, *Breaking the Mold*.

22. Harrington, *Care and Equality*; Joyce K. Fletcher, *Disappearing Acts: Gender, Power, and Relational Practice at Work* (Cambridge, Mass.: MIT Press, 1999); Williams, *Unbending Gender*.

23. A particularly useful resource for all these sources comes from the "workfam" newsgroup (http://lsir.la.psu.edu/workfam), compiled at Pennsylvania State University, itself an important player in the field.

24. There are also European organizations concerned with these issues. In Britain, for example, there are the Work-Life Research Centre, the government Work-Home Balance Project, the National Work-Life Forum, and Demos. In the Netherlands, the ROC, a large school in Amsterdam with thirty thousand students and three thousand teachers, launched a pilot "work and life in balance" program with two teacher teams, in connection with a major reorganization in 2000–01.

25. See Ford Foundation, *Work and Family Responsibilities: Achieving A Balance* (New York: Ford Foundation, 1989), and Ford Foundation, *Men and Women at Home and in the Workplace: Current Debates and Future Directions* (New York: Ford Foundation, 1989).

26. Rapoport and others, *Relinking Life and Work.*

27. Peter Senge, *The Fifth Discipline: The Art and Practice of the Learning Organization* (New York: Doubleday, 1990); Peter Senge and others, *The Dance of Change: The Challenges to Sustaining Momentum in Learning Organizations: A Fifth Discipline Resource* (New York: Doubleday, 1999).

28. Rapoport and others, *Relinking Life and Work*; Bailyn, Fletcher, and Kolb, "Unexpected Connections."

29. CIMMYT is the Centro International de Mejoramiento de Maiz y Trigo [International Center for Improvement of Maize and Wheat], based in Mexico; BRAC originally stood for the Bangladesh Rural Advancement Committee. The CIMMYT, BRAC, and Body Shop cases all appear as chapters in Aruna Rao, Rieky Stuart, and David Kelleher (eds.), *Gender at Work: Organizational Change for Equality* (West Hartford, Conn.: Kumarian Press, 1999): Deborah Merrill-Sands, Joyce K. Fletcher, and Anne Acosta, "Engendering Organizational Change: A Case Study of Strengthening Gender-Equity and

Organizational Effectiveness in an International Agricultural Research Institute"; Aruna Rao, Reiky Stuart, and David Kelleher, "Building Gender Capital at BRAC: A Case Study"; and Deborah M. Kolb and Debra E. Meyerson, "Keeping Gender in the Plot: A Case Study of The Body Shop." See also the following case studies in Jill Casner-Lotto (ed.), *Holding a Job, Having a Life: Strategies for Change* (Scarsdale, N.Y.: Work in America Institute, 2000): Lotte Bailyn, Dale Bengtsen, Françoise Carré, and Mark Tierney, "The Radcliffe-Fleet Work and Life Integration Project"; Barbara Miller and Jerry Cashman, "Hewlett-Packard/Agilent Technologies: Linking Business Challenges and Work/Life Needs Through 'Reinventing Work'"; Mary B. Young, "The Work Group Action Planning Process at Merck & Company"; and Sandy M. Sindell and Perry Christensen, "Bank of America's Dual Agenda: Improving Both Business and Work/Life Balance Through Work Redesign."

Chapter Two

1. As historian Nancy Cott notes, "Women depended on men to buy and work land and produce grain, but men had no bread without women baking it." Nancy F. Cott, *The Bonds of Womanhood: "Woman's Sphere" in New England, 1780–1835* (New Haven, Conn.: Yale University Press, 1977), p. 22. See also John Demos, *Past, Present, and Personal: The Family and the Life Course in American History* (New York: Oxford University Press, 1986), pp, 43–45.

2. Cott, *The Bonds of Womanhood*; Demos, *Past, Present, and Personal*; see also Steven Mintz and Susan Kellogg, *Domestic Revolutions: A Social History of Family Life* (New York: Free Press, 1988), for an overview of this transition; and Williams, *Unbending Gender*.

3. See Sharon Hays, *The Cultural Contradictions of Motherhood* (New Haven, Conn.: Yale University Press, 1996).

4. Demos, *Past, Present, and Personal,* p. 61, notes the importance of the coincidence of the rise of large bureaucratic organizations and suburbanization on the changing role of fathers. See also "The Golden Age: Families of the 1950s," in Mintz and Kellogg, *Domestic Revolutions.*

5. Williams, *Unbending Gender,* illuminates the sources and influence of these underlying assumptions in her discussion of the ideal worker and its relation to the ideology of domesticity, pp. 20–31. See also Rhona Rapoport and Robert N. Rapoport, "Changing Family Structure: Toward Equality of Opportunity and Constraint," paper presented to the United Nations Interregional Seminar on the Family in a Changing Society (London, 1973), p. 23, on the phenomenon of a "work ethic . . . that has an insatiability attached to it, particularly in relation to males."

6. Kanter describes a "masculine ethic" in the writing about managers that tacitly "elevates the traits assumed to belong to men with educational advantages to necessities for effective organizations." Quoted in Joan Acker, "Hierarchies, Jobs, Bodies: A Theory of Gendered Organizations," *Gender and Society,* 1999, 4, 143.

7. Bailyn, *Breaking the Mold,* pp. 105–113, examines the issue of commitment in depth.

8. Mary Beth Grover, "Daddy Stress," *Forbes,* Sept. 6, 1999, pp. 202–208.

9. Ruth Shalit, "The Taming of the Shrews," *Elle,* Aug. 2001, pp. 102–109.

10. See Robert Bly, *Iron John: A Book About Men* (Reading, Mass.: Addison-Wesley, 1990), and Robert Moore and Douglas Gillette, *King, Warrior, Magician, Lover: Rediscovering the Archetypes of the Mature Masculine* (New York: Harper-Collins, 1990).

11. Virginia Valian, *Why So Slow? The Advancement of Women* (Cambridge, Mass.: MIT Press, 1997), p. 20.

12. For an interesting exception, see Rochelle Sharpe, "As Leaders, Women Rule," *Business Week*, Nov. 20, 2000, pp. 75–84. Of particular interest is the boxed information at the end of the article, titled "What Can Men Do?" which addresses the issue of men's lack of relational skills. See also Francine Russo, "Aggression Loses Some of Its Punch," *Time*, July 30, 2001, pp. 42–44.

13. For more on the concept of how relational practice "gets disappeared" in the workplace, see Fletcher, *Disappearing Acts*.

14. See Karl E. Weick, "Small Wins: Redefining the Scale of Social Problems," *American Psychologist*, 1984, 39(1), 40–49.

15. See Joyce K. Fletcher and Lotte Bailyn, "Challenging the Last Boundary: Reconnecting Work and Family," in Michael B. Arthur and Denise M. Rousseau (eds.), *The Boundaryless Career: A New Employment Principle for a New Organizational Era* (Oxford: Oxford University Press, 1996).

Chapter Three

1. When we speak of performance, we are not, of course, referring only to a financial bottom line. We have found the tendency to see gender equity and performance as dichotomous and adversarial to be as prevalent in nonprofits as it is in for-profit organizations.

2. Rapoport and others, *Relinking Life and Work*, pp. 22–24; Bailyn, Fletcher, and Kolb, "Unexpected Connections"; Rhona Rapoport, Lotte Bailyn, Deborah M. Kolb, and Joyce K. Fletcher, "Relinking Life and Work," *Systems Thinker*, 1998, 9(8), 1–5; Deborah M. Kolb and Deborah Merrill-Sands, "Waiting for Outcomes: Anchoring a Dual Agenda for Change in Cultural Assumptions," *Women in Management Review*, 1999, 14, 194–202.

3. See Kolb and Merrill-Sands, "Waiting for Outcomes," for an extended discussion of this case.

4. See Miller and Cashman, "Hewlett-Packard/Agilent Technologies."

5. Merrill-Sands, Fletcher, and Acosta, "Engendering Organizational Change."

6. For a full report on the work from which this case is drawn, see Kolb and Meyerson, "Keeping Gender in the Plot." For a number of insights drawn from this project, see three articles published in a special edition of *Organization*, 2000, 7(4): Gill Coleman and Ann Rippin, "Putting Feminist Theory to Work: Collaboration as a Means Toward Organizational Change," pp. 573–588; Robin J. Ely and Debra E. Meyerson, "Advancing Gender Equity in Organizations: The Challenge and Importance of Maintaining a Gender Narrative," pp. 589–608; and Debra E. Meyerson and Deborah M. Kolb, "Moving Out of the Armchair: Developing a Framework to Bridge the Gap Between Feminist Theory and Practice," pp. 553–572. On the concept of "disappearing" contributions, Joyce Fletcher, in *Disappearing Acts*, explains that because of gender expectations, when women exhibit relational skills, these behaviors are more likely to be seen as natural attributes and less likely to be seen as evidence of competence or skill.

7. For more on collaborative interaction as a mode of intervention, see "Research Philosophy and Methods," in Rhona Rapoport and Robert N. Rapoport, *Dual-Career Families Reexamined: New Integrations of Work and Family* (New York: HarperCollins, 1976), and Barbara Laslett and Rhona Rapoport, "Collaborative Interviewing and Interactive Research," *Journal of Marriage and the Family*, Nov. 1975, pp. 968–977. For more on relational theory, see Jean Baker Miller, *Toward a New Psychology of Women* (Boston: Beacon Press, 1976), and Jean Baker Miller and Irene Pierce Stiver, *The Healing Connection: How Women Form Relationships in Therapy and in Life* (Boston: Beacon Press, 1997). For more on how relational theory is challenging gendered norms about learning and achievement in the workplace, see Fletcher, *Disappearing Acts*.

Chapter Four

1. Robert Rapoport provided the most widely cited definition: "Action research aims to contribute both to the practical concerns of people in an immediate problematic situation and to the goals of social science by joint collaboration within a mutually acceptable ethical framework." See Robert N. Rapoport, "Three Dilemmas in Action Research," *Human Relations*, 1970, 23, 499–513. There are a number of useful overviews of the development and varieties of action research: Max Elden and Rupert F. Chisholm, "Emerging Varieties of Action Research: Introduction to the Special Edition," *Human Relations*, 1993, 46, 121–142; Colin Eden and Chris Huxham, "Action Research for the Study of Organizations," in Stewart R. Clegg, Cynthia Hardy, and Walter R. Nord (eds.), *Handbook of Organization Studies* (London: Sage, 1996); Joe Raelin, "Preface" [to a special edition on action research methods], *Management Learning*, 1999, 30, 115–125; Peter Reason (ed.), *Participation in Human Inquiry* (London: Sage, 1994); Stephen Kemmis and Robin McTaggart, "Participative Action Research," in Norman Denzin and Yvonna S. Lincoln (eds.), *Handbook of Qualitative Research*, 2nd ed. (Thousand Oaks, Calif.: Sage, 2000); and Peter Reason and Hilary Bradbury (eds.), *Handbook of Action Research: Participative Inquiry and Practice* (London: Sage, 2001). See also Chris Argyris, Robert Putnam, and Diana McLain Smith, *Action Science: Concepts, Methods, and Skills for Research and Intervention* (San Francisco: Jossey-Bass, 1985); William F. Whyte, Davydd J. Greenwood, and Peter Lazes (eds.), *Participatory Action Research* (Thousand Oaks, Calif.: Sage, 1991); and Davydd J. Greenwood and Morten Levin, *Introduction to Action Research: Social Research for Social Changes* (Thousand Oaks, Calif.: Sage, 1998).

2. See, for example, two books by Edgar H. Schein: *Organizational Culture and Leadership,* 2nd ed. (San Francisco: Jossey-Bass, 1992), and *Process Consultation Revisited: Building the Helping Relationship* (Reading, Mass.: Addison-Wesley, 1999).

3. Suggested readings to distribute for background: Rapoport and others, *Relinking Life and Work*; Bailyn, Fletcher, and Kolb, "Unexpected Connections"; Rapoport, Bailyn, Kolb, and Fletcher, "Relinking Life and Work"; Debra E. Meyerson and Joyce K. Fletcher, "A Modest Manifesto for Shattering the Glass Ceiling," *Harvard Business Review*, 2000, 78(1), 127–136; and Bailyn, *Breaking the Mold*.

4. Maureen A. Harvey, personal communication, 1998.

5. For more information on how to negotiate entry in a way that takes account of the gender dynamics inherent in any negotiation process, see Deborah M. Kolb and Judith Williams, *The Shadow Negotiation: How Women Can Master the Hidden Agendas That Determine Bargaining Success* (New York: Simon & Schuster, 2000).

6. This case is based on an unpublished report prepared by Maureen A. Harvey for LUME International, LLP.

7. For an additional case study that documents the analysis process in detail, see Merrill-Sands, Fletcher, and Acosta, "Engendering Organizational Change."

8. Maureen A. Harvey, personal communication, Feb. 19, 1999.

9. This iterative feedback process is described in Merrill-Sands, Fletcher, and Acosta, "Engendering Organizational Change."

10. Unpublished report prepared by Joyce K. Fletcher for LUME International, LLP.

11. Kolb and Merrill-Sands, "Waiting for Outcomes."

12. Deborah Merrill-Sands, working with consultants from Training Resources Group in Washington, D.C., made a significant contribution to the method through the design of small group working sessions to be used after the general feedback plenary session. See Merrill-Sands, Fletcher, and Acosta, "Engendering Organizational Change," for more information on the design and use of these small groups.

Chapter Five

1. On "small wins" and "strategic failures," see Weick, "Small Wins," and Sim B. Sitkin, "Learning Through Failure: The Strategy of Small Losses," *Research in Organizational Behavior*, 1992, *14*, 231–266. See also Meyerson and Fletcher, "A Modest Manifesto."

2. See Fletcher and Bailyn, "Challenging the Last Boundary."

3. For more on the concept of "honoring" resistance, see Miller and Stiver, *The Healing Connection*, pp. 147–163.

4. This case is also described in Rapoport and others, *Relinking Life and Work*; Leslie A. Perlow, *Finding Time: How Corporations, Individuals, and Families Can Benefit from New Work Practices* (Ithaca, N.Y.: Cornell University Press, 1997); and Leslie A. Perlow, Rhona Rapoport, Deborah M. Kolb, and Lotte Bailyn, "Working with Resistance: Notes on Changing Organizations to Enhance Gender Equity," paper presented at the annual meeting of the Academy of Management, Dallas, Tex., Aug. 1994.

5. Quoted in Perlow, *Finding Time*, p. 135.

6. See Lotte Bailyn, Paula M. Rayman, Maureen A. Harvey, Robert Krim, Robert Read, Françoise Carré, Jillian Dickert, Pamela Joshi, and Alina Martinez, *The Radcliffe-Fleet Project: Creating Work and Life Integration Solutions* (Cambridge, Mass.: Radcliffe Public Policy Institute, 1998); Paula M. Rayman, *Beyond the Bottom Line: The Search for Dignity at Work* (New York: Bedford/St. Martin's, 2001); and Bailyn, Bengtsen, Carré, and Tierney, "The Radcliffe-Fleet Work and Life Integration Project."

7. Reported at the National Advisory Council for Holding a Job, Having a Life, of the Work in American Institute, White Plains, N.Y., Dec. 5, 2000.

8. Quoted in Bailyn, Bengtsen, Carré, and Tierney, "The Radcliffe-Fleet Work and Life Integration Project," p. 40.

Chapter Six

1. Judith V. Jordan, Alexandra Kaplan, Jean B. Miller, Irene P. Stiver, and Janet Surrey (eds.), *Women's Growth in Connection* (New York: Guilford Press, 1991).
2. Miller and Stiver, *The Healing Connection.*

Chapter Seven

1. We would like to acknowledge the assistance provided by Ann Rippen, Jan Jaffe, Maureen A. Harvey, and Roy Jacques in framing and thinking through the issue of diffusion.
2. For other ideas on diffusion of organizational change, see "The Challenges of Sustaining Transformation" in Senge and others, *The Dance of Change,* ch. 7–9.
3. See David Kelleher and Kirsten Moore, *Marginal to Mainstream: Scaling Up Gender and Organizational Change Interventions* (Boston: Center for Gender in Organizations, Simmons Graduate School of Management, 1997).
4. David T. Kearns and David A. Nadler, *Prophets in the Dark: How Xerox Reinvented Itself and Beat Back the Japanese* (New York: HarperBusiness, 1992); Gary Jacobson and John Hillkirk, *Xerox: American Samurai* (New York: Collier, 1986).
5. Kolb and Merrill-Sands, "Waiting for Outcomes."
6. Rapoport and others, *Relinking Life and Work,* p. 23.
7. Kolb and Merrill-Sands, "Waiting for Outcomes," p. 199.
8. See the discussion of narrative in Kolb and Merrill-Sands,

"Waiting for Outcomes"; Ely and Meyerson, "Advancing Gender Equity in Organizations"; and Robin J. Ely and Debra E. Meyerson, "Theories of Gender in Organizations: A New Approach to Organizational Analysis and Change," in Barry Staw and Robert Sutton (eds.), *Research in Organizational Behavior*, 2000, 22, 105–153.

9. Ann Rippin, "Dripping Ink into a Pool: Some Practical Experiences of Diffusing Change," unpublished paper, 1999.

10. Rippin, "Dripping Ink into a Pool."

11. Kolb and Merrill-Sands, "Waiting for Outcomes," pp. 199–200.

12. Kolb and Merrill-Sands, "Waiting for Outcomes," p. 200.

13. Merrill-Sands, Fletcher, and Acosta, "Engendering Organizational Change," p. 121.

14. Kolb and Meyerson, "Keeping Gender in the Plot"; Meyerson and Fletcher, "A Modest Manifesto"; Ely and Meyerson, "Theories of Gender in Organizations."

Chapter Eight

1. Arlie Hochschild, *The Time Bind: When Work Becomes Home and Home Becomes Work* (New York: Metropolitan Books, 1997).

2. Sharpe, "As Leaders, Women Rule," p. 76.

3. Anand Swamy, Young Lee, Stephen Knack, and Omar Azfar, *Gender and Corruption* (College Park: Center for Institutional Reform and the Informal Sector, University of Maryland, Apr. 1999), p. 19.

4. Jessica DeGroot, e-mail, Apr. 4, 2001.

5. See, for example, Keith H. Hammonds, "Family Values," *Fast Company*, Dec. 2000, pp. 169–182.

6. June Zeitlin, "Gender and Institutional Change Project Report and Recommendations," unpublished report submitted to the Ford Foundation, July 1999, p. 6.

Appendix

1. Rhona Rapoport, personal communication, Sept. 23, 1998; and Robert N. Rapoport and Rhona Rapoport, "Work and Family in Contemporary Society," *American Sociological Review*, 1965, 30, 381.

2. See Rapoport and Rapoport, *Dual-Career Families*; Rapoport and Rapoport, *Dual-Career Families Reexamined*; and Robert N. Rapoport and Rhona Rapoport. "Dual-Career Families: The Evolution of a Concept," in Eric Trist and Hugh Murray (eds.), *The Social Engagement of Social Science: A Tavistock Anthology* (Philadelphia: University of Pennsylvania Press, 1989).

3. Quote from Rapoport and Rapoport, "Changing Family Structure," p. 23; see also Rhona Rapoport and Robert N. Rapoport, "Men, Women, and Equity," *Family Coordinator*, Oct. 1975, pp. 421-432.

4. Rhona Rapoport, "Restructuring Work and Family," *Proceedings of the Einar Thorsrud Memorial Symposium* (Oslo: Work Research Institute, 1987); Rhona Rapoport with Peter Moss, *Men and Women as Equals at Work* (London: Thomas Coram Research Unit, 1990); and Rhona Rapoport, "Men's Involvement as Fathers in the Care of Children: Possibilities of Change in the Workplace," *European Childcare Network Services*, 1990.

5. Rapoport and Rapoport, "Research Philosophy and Methods"; Laslett and Rapoport, "Collaborative Interviewing and Interactive Research."

6. Bailyn, "Notes on the Role of Choice."

7. Rhona Rapoport, personal communication, Sept. 23, 1998.

8. See Lotte Bailyn, "Career and Family Orientations of Husbands and Wives in Relation to Marital Happiness," *Human Relations*, 1970, 23, 97–113, and Lotte Bailyn, "Family Constraints on Women's Work," *Annals of the New York Academy of Science*, 1973, 208, 82–90.

9. See Lotte Bailyn, "Issues of Work and Family in Organizations: Responding to Social Diversity," in Michael B. Arthur, Lotte Bailyn, Daniel J. Levinson, and Herbert A. Shepard, *Working with Careers* (New York: Center for Research in Career Development, Columbia University, 1984); Lotte Bailyn, "Experiencing Technical Work: A Comparison of Male and Female Engineers, *Human Relations*, 1987, 40, 299–312; and Lotte Bailyn, "Changing the Conditions of Work: Responding to Increasing Work Force Diversity and New Family Patterns," in Thomas A. Kochan and Michael Useem (eds.), *Transforming Organizations* (Oxford: Oxford University Press, 1992).

10. Lotte Bailyn, "Toward the Perfect Workplace?" *Communications of the ACM*, 1989, 460–471.

11. Bailyn, *Breaking the Mold*, p. xii.

12. See Rapoport and others, *Relinking Life and Work*, p 3.

13. James A. Levine, Dana E. Friedman, and Ellen Galinsky, "Work-Family Collaborative Research Project at Corning, Inc.," unpublished report submitted to the Ford Foundation, Jan. 2, 1995.

14. Barbara Miller and others, "Relinking Life and Livelihood: A Primer for Individual and Organizational Change," unpublished report submitted to the Ford Foundation, May 1996; Roy Jacques, "Final Report Regarding the Artemis/Ford Foundation Tandem Research," unpublished report submitted to the Ford Foundation, Mar. 1996.

15. Lotte Bailyn and Deborah M. Kolb, "Work/Family Project at Xerox," proposal submitted to the Ford Foundation, 1991, p. 7.

16. Deborah M. Kolb, personal communication, Apr. 7, 1999. See also, Kolb and Williams, *The Shadow Negotiation*.

17. See the following by Leslie A. Perlow: "The Time Famine: The Unintended Consequence of the Way Time Is Used at Work," doctoral dissertation, Massachusetts Institute of Technology, 1995; *Finding Time;* "Boundary Control: The Social Ordering of Work and Family Time in a High-Tech Corporation," *Administrative Science Quarterly,* 1998, 43, 328–357; and "The Time Famine: Toward a Sociology of Work Time," *Administrative Science Quarterly,* 1999, 44, 57–81.

18. Robin D. Johnson, "Where's the Power in Empowerment? Definition, Differences, and Dilemmas of Empowerment in the Context of Work-Family Boundary Management," doctoral dissertation, Harvard University, 1994.

19. Deborah M. Kolb, personal communication. Quotes from Fletcher, *Disappearing Acts,* p. 9, and Joyce K. Fletcher, personal communication, Mar. 29, 1999. See also Deborah M. Kolb, "Women's Work: Peacemaking in Organizations," in Deborah M. Kolb and Jean M. Bartunek (eds.), *Hidden Conflict in Organizations: Uncovering Behind-the-Scenes Disputes* (Thousand Oaks, Calif.: Sage, 1992). Related publications by Joyce K. Fletcher include "Toward a Theory of Relational Practice in Organizations: A Feminist Reconstruction of 'Real' Work," doctoral dissertation, Boston University, 1994; "Personal Development in the New Organization: A Relational Approach to Developing the Protean Worker," in Douglas T. Hall (ed.), *The Career Is Dead—Long Live the Career* (San Francisco: Jossey Bass, 1996); and "Relational Practice: A Feminist Reconstruction of Work," *Journal of Management Inquiry,* 1998, 7, 163–186.

20. Rapoport and Rapoport, "Men, Women, and Equity," p. 424.

21. Career facts from Maureen A. Harvey, personal communication, Feb. 17, 1999.

22. Lotte Bailyn and others, "Work-Family: A Catalyst for Change," unpublished report to the Ford Foundation, Sept. 1993.

23. Rapoport and others, *Relinking Life and Work,* pp. 3–4. See also Bailyn, Fletcher, and Kolb, "Unexpected Connections."

24. Zeitlin, "Gender and Institutional Change Project Report and Recommendations," p. 18.

25. See Ellen Galinsky, *Ask the Children* (New York: Quill, 2000); Levine and Pittinsky, *Working Fathers*; and the FWI Web site (http://www.familesandworkinst.org).

26. See Miller and Cashman, "Hewlett-Packard/Agilent Technologies," p. 77.

27. Lotte Bailyn and others, *The Radcliffe-Fleet Project*; Rayman and others, "Designing Organizational Solutions to Integrate Work and Life"; Rayman, *Beyond the Bottom Line*.

28. Casner-Lotto, *Holding a Job, Having a Life*, p. v.

29. Lotte Bailyn and Thomas A. Kochan, "Proposal to Create a Workplace Center at MIT to Advance Institutional Change for Working Families," proposal submitted to the Alfred P. Sloan Foundation, May 14, 2001.

30. Personal communication from Ragnhild Sohlberg, Aug. 13, 2001, and see Charles Fishman, "The Way to Enough," *Fast Company*, June 1999, pp. 160–175. Personal communications from Louise Boelens, July 3, 2001; Shirley Dex, July 28, 2001; and Suzan Lewis, July 20, 2001.

31. See Deborah M. Kolb, Joyce K. Fletcher, Debra E. Meyerson, Deborah Merrill-Sands, and Robin J. Ely, *Making Change: A Framework for Promoting Gender Equity in Organizations*. (Boston: Center for Gender in Organizations, Simmons Graduate School of Management, 1998); Meyerson and Kolb, "Moving Out of the Armchair"; Kolb and Meyerson, "Keeping Gender in the Plot"; Ely and Meyerson, "Advancing Gender Equity in Organizations"; and Ely and Meyerson, "Theories of Gender in Organizations."

32. See Ely and Meyerson, "Advancing Gender Equity in Organizations"; Ely and Meyerson, "Theories of Gender in Organizations"; Coleman and Rippin, "Putting Feminist Theory to Work"; and Meyerson and Kolb, "Moving Out of the Armchair." Thanks to Debra Meyerson (personal communication,

Aug.8, 2001) for pointing out the significance of the findings on changing how people think and talk.

33. Gill Coleman, personal communication, July 22, 2001.

34. Deborah Merrill-Sands, personal communication, May 20, 1999. See Kolb and Merrill-Sands, "Waiting for Outcomes," and Merrill-Sands, Fletcher, and Acosta, "Engendering Organizational Change."

35. Quotations from the pamphlet *Gender, Leadership, and Organizational Effectiveness: Working at the Intersection of Scholarship and Practice* (Boston: Center for Gender in Organizations, Simmons Graduate School of Management, n.d.).

36. See the CGO Web site, http://www.simmons.edu/gsm/cgo.

37. Debra E. Meyerson and Maureen Scully, *Tempered Radicalism: Changing the Workplace from Within* (Boston: Center for Gender in Organizations, Simmons Graduate School of Management, 1999). See also Debra E. Meyerson, *Tempered Radicals: How People Use Difference to Inspire Change at Work* (Boston: Harvard Business School Press, 2001), and Keith H. Hammonds, "Practical Radicals," *Fast Company*, Sept. 2000, pp. 162–174.

38. See Joyce K. Fletcher and Roy Jacques, *Relational Practice: An Emerging Stream of Theory and Its Significance* (Boston: Center for Gender in Organizations, Simmons Graduate School of Management, 1999); Joyce K. Fletcher, Jean Baker Miller and Judith V. Jordan, "Women and the Workplace: Applications of the Psychodynamic Theory," *American Journal of Psychoanalysis*, 2000, 60, 243–262; and Joyce K. Fletcher, *Relational Theory in the Workplace* (Wellesley, Mass.: Stone Center, Wellesley Centers for Women, Wellesley College, 1996).

39. Center for Gender in Organizations, *Gender at Work: Beyond White, Western, Middle-Class, Heterosexual, Professional Women* (Boston: Center for Gender in Organizations, Simmons Graduate School of Management, 2000). See also Robin J. Ely and Debra E. Meyerson, "Moving from Gender

to Diversity in Organizational Diagnosis and Intervention," *Diversity Factor*, 1999, 7(3), 28–33.

40. Massachusetts Institute of Technology, *A Study on the Status of Women Faculty in Science at MIT* (Cambridge, Mass.: Massachusetts Institute of Technology, 1999), available at http://web.mit.edu/fnl/women/women.html.

41. See also two op-ed pieces by Shirley M. Tilghman: "Science vs. the Female Scientist," *New York Times*, Jan. 25, 1993, and "Science vs. Women: A Radical Solution," *New York Times*, Jan. 26, 1993.

42. For example, Maureen A. Harvey, *Work-Life Redesign at DTE Energy* (Scarsdale, N.Y.: Work in America Institute, 2001).

43. Bailyn, Fletcher, and Kolb, "Unexpected Connections;" Meyerson and Fletcher, "A Modest Manifesto."

Published Reports of Dual Agenda Experiments and Additional References

Dual Agenda Reports

Bailyn, Lotte. "The Impact of Corporate Culture on Work-Family Integration." In Saroj Parasuraman and Jeffrey H. Greenhaus (eds.), *Work and Family in a Changing World: A Multiple Stakeholder Perspective.* Westport, Conn.: Quorum, 1997.

Bailyn, Lotte, Dale Bengtsen, Françoise Carré, and Mark Tierney, "The Radcliffe-Fleet Work and Life Integration Project." In Jill Casner-Lotto, *Holding a Job, Having a Life: Strategies for Change.* Scarsdale, N.Y.: Work in America Institute, 2000.

Bailyn, Lotte, Joyce K. Fletcher, and Deborah M. Kolb. "Unexpected Connections: Considering Employees' Personal Lives

Can Revitalize Your Business. *Sloan Management Review,* 1997, 38(4), 11–19.

Bailyn, Lotte, Rhona Rapoport, Deborah M. Kolb, Joyce K. Fletcher, Dana E. Friedman, Susan Eaton, Maureen A. Harvey, and Barbara Miller. "Relinking Work and Family: A Catalyst for Organizational Change." In Miguel Pina e Cunha and Carlos Alves (eds.), *Readings in Organizations Science: Organizational Change in a Changing Context.* Lisbon, Portugal: Instituto Superior de Psicologia Aplicada, 1999.

Bailyn, Lotte, Rhona Rapoport, and Joyce K. Fletcher. "Moving Corporations in the U.S. Toward Gender Equity: A Cautionary Tale." In Linda Haas (ed.), *Organizational Change and Gender Equity: International Perspectives on Fathers and Mothers at the Workplace.* Thousand Oaks, Calif.: Sage, 2000.

Bailyn, Lotte, Paula M. Rayman, Maureen Harvey, Robert Krim, Robert Read, Françoise Carré, Jillian Dickert, Pamela Joshi, and Alina Martinez. *The Radcliffe-Fleet Project: Creating Work and Life Integration Solutions.* Cambridge, Mass.: Radcliffe Public Policy Institute, 1998.

Coleman, Gill, and Ann Rippin, "Putting Feminist Theory to Work: Collaboration as a Means Toward Organizational Change." *Organization,* 2000, 7(4), 573–588.

Ely, Robin J., and Debra E. Meyerson, "Advancing Gender Equity in Organizations: The Challenge and Importance of Maintaining a Gender Narrative." *Organization,* 2000, 7(4), 589–608.

Fletcher, Joyce K., and Lotte Bailyn. "Challenging the Last Boundary: Reconnecting Work and Family." In Michael B. Arthur and Denise M. Rousseau (eds.), *The Boundaryless Career: A New Employment Principle for a New Organizational Era.* Oxford: Oxford University Press, 1996.

Fletcher, Joyce K., and Rhona Rapoport. "Work-Family Issues as a Catalyst for Change." In Suzan Lewis and Jeremy Lewis (eds.), *Rethinking Employment: The Work-Family Challenge.* London: Sage, 1996.

Harvey, Maureen A. *Work-Life Redesign at DTE Energy.* Scarsdale, N.Y.: Work in America Institute, 2001.

Johnson, Robin D. "Where's the Power in Empowerment? Definition, Differences, and Dilemmas of Empowerment in the Context of Work-Family Boundary Management." Doctoral dissertation, Harvard University, 1994.

Kolb, Deborah M., and Deborah Merrill-Sands. "Waiting for Outcomes: Anchoring a Dual Agenda for Change to Cultural Assumptions." *Women in Management Review,* 1999, *14,* 194–202.

Kolb, Deborah M., and Debra E. Meyerson. "Keeping Gender in the Plot: A Case Study of The Body Shop." In Aruna Rao, Rieky Stuart, and David Kelleher (eds.), *Gender at Work: Organizational Change for Equality.* West Hartford, Conn.: Kumarian Press, 1999.

Merrill-Sands, Deborah, Joyce K. Fletcher, and Anne Acosta. "Engendering Organizational Change: A Case Study of Strengthening Gender-Equity and Organizational Effectiveness in an International Agricultural Research Institute." In Aruna Rao, Rieky Stuart, and David Kelleher (eds.), *Gender at Work: Organizational Change for Equality.* West Hartford, Conn.: Kumarian Press, 1999.

Meyerson, Debra E., and Deborah M. Kolb, "Moving Out of the Armchair: Developing a Framework to Bridge the Gap Between Feminist Theory and Practice." *Organization,* 2000, *7*(4), 553–572.

Miller, Barbara, and Jerry Cashman. "Hewlett-Packard/Agilent Technologies: Linking Business Challenges and Work/Life Needs Through 'Reinventing Work.'" In Jill Casner-Lotto (ed.), *Holding a Job, Having a Life: Strategies for Change.* Scarsdale, N.Y.: Work in America Institute, 2000.

Perlow, Leslie A. *Finding Time: How Corporations, Individuals, and Families Can Benefit from New Work Practices.* Ithaca, N.Y.: Cornell University Press, 1997.

Perlow, Leslie A. "Boundary Control: The Social Ordering of Work and Family Time in a High-Tech Corporation." *Administrative Science Quarterly*, 1998, *43*, 328–357.

Perlow, Leslie A. "The Time Famine: Toward a Sociology of Work Time." *Administrative Science Quarterly*, 1999, *44*, 57–81.

Rapoport, Rhona, Lotte Bailyn, Deborah M. Kolb, Joyce Fletcher, Dana E. Friedman, Susan Eaton, Maureen A. Harvey, and Barbara Miller. *Relinking Life and Work: Toward a Better Future*. New York: Ford Foundation, 1996; Waltham, Mass: Pegasus Communications, 1998.

Rayman, Paula M., Lotte Bailyn, Jillian Dickert, and Françoise Carré (with Maureen A. Harvey, Robert Krim, and Robert Read). "Designing Organizational Solutions to Integrate Work and Life." *Women in Management Review*. 1999, *14*, 164–176.

Sindell, Sandy M., and Perry Christensen. "Bank of America's Dual Agenda: Improving Both Business and Work/Life Balance Through Work Redesign." In Jill Casner-Lotto (ed.), *Holding a Job, Having a Life: Strategies for Change*. Scarsdale, N.Y.: Work in America Institute, 2000.

Young, Mary B. "The Work Group Action Planning Process at Merck & Company." In Jill Casner-Lotto (ed.), *Holding a Job, Having a Life: Strategies for Change*. Scarsdale, N.Y.: Work in America Institute, 2000.

Additional References

Acker, Joan, "Hierarchies, Jobs, Bodies: A Theory of Gendered Organizations." *Gender and Society*, 1999, *4*, 139–158.

Argyris, Chris, Robert Putnam, and Diana McLain Smith. *Action Science: Concepts, Methods, and Skills for Research and Intervention*. San Francisco: Jossey-Bass, 1985.

Arthur, Michael B., and Denise M. Rousseau (eds.). *The Boundaryless Career: A New Employment Principle for a New Organizational Era*. Oxford: Oxford University Press, 1996.

Bailyn, Lotte, "Notes on the Role of Choice in the Psychology of Professional Women." *Daedalus*, 1964, 94, 700–710.

Bailyn, Lotte. "Career and Family Orientations of Husbands and Wives in Relation to Marital Happiness." *Human Relations*, 1970, 23, 97–113.

Bailyn, Lotte. "Family Constraints on Women's Work." *Annals of the New York Academy of Science*, 1973, 208, 82–90.

Bailyn, Lotte. "Issues of Work and Family in Organizations: Responding to Social Diversity." In Michael B. Arthur, Lotte Bailyn, Daniels J. Levinson, and Herbert A. Shepard, *Working with Careers*. New York: Center for Research in Career Development, Columbia University, 1984.

Bailyn, Lotte. "Experiencing Technical Work: A Comparison of Male and Female Engineers." *Human Relations*, 1987, 40, 299–312.

Bailyn, Lotte, "Toward the Perfect Workplace?" *Communications of the ACM*, 1989, 460–471.

Bailyn, Lotte. "Changing the Conditions of Work: Responding to Increasing Work Force Diversity and New Family Patterns." In Thomas A. Kochan and Michael Useem (eds.), *Transforming Organizations*. Oxford: Oxford University Press, 1992.

Bailyn, Lotte. *Breaking the Mold: Women, Men, and Time in the New Corporate World*. New York: Free Press, 1993.

Berke, Richard L. "Bush Is Providing Corporate Model for White House." *New York Times on the Web*, Mar. 11, 2001.

Bly, Robert. *Iron John: A Book About Men*. Reading, Mass.: Addison-Wesley, 1990.

Carelli, Richard. "Work Isn't All, Rehnquist Tells Law School Graduates." *Boston Globe*, May 29, 2000, p. A10.

Casner-Lotto, Jill (ed.). *Holding a Job, Having a Life: Strategies for Change*. Scarsdale, N.Y.: Work in America Institute, 2000.

Center for Gender in Organizations. *Gender at Work: Beyond White, Western, Middle-Class, Heterosexual, Professional*

Women. Boston: Center for Gender in Organizations, Simmons Graduate School of Management, 2000.

Center for Policy Alternatives and Lifetime Television. "Women's Voices 2000: The Most Comprehensive Polling and Research Project on Women's Values and Policy Priorities for the Economy." http://www.stateaction.org, 2000.

Cott, Nancy F. *The Bonds of Womanhood: "Woman's Sphere" in New England, 1780–1835.* New Haven, Conn.: Yale University Press, 1977.

Dahlström, Edmund, and Rita Liljeström. *The Changing Roles of Men and Women.* London: Duckworth, 1967.

Demos, John, *Past, Present, and Personal: The Family and the Life Course in American History.* New York: Oxford University Press, 1986.

Eden, Colin, and Chris Huxham. "Action Research for the Study of Organizations." In Stewart R. Clegg, Cynthia Hardy, and Walter R. Nord (eds.), *Handbook of Organization Studies.* London: Sage, 1996.

Elden, Max, and Rupert F. Chisholm. "Emerging Varieties of Action Research: Introduction to the Special Edition." *Human Relations,* 1993, 46, 121–142.

Ely, Robin J., and Debra E. Meyerson. "Moving from Gender to Diversity in Organizational Diagnosis and Intervention." *Diversity Factor,* 1999, 7(3), 28–33.

Ely, Robin J., and Debra E. Meyerson. "Theories of Gender in Organizations: A New Approach to Organizational Analysis and Change." In Barry Staw and Robert Sutton (eds.), *Research in Organizational Behavior,* 2000, 22, 105–153

Ferber, Marianne A., and Julie A. Nelson (eds.). *Beyond Economic Man: Feminist Theory and Economics.* Chicago: University of Chicago Press, 1993.

Fishman, Charles. "Sanity Inc." *Fast Company,* Jan. 1999, pp. 84–96.

Fishman, Charles. "The Way to Enough." *Fast Company*, June 1999, pp. 160–175.

Fletcher, Joyce K. "Castrating the Female Advantage: Feminist Standpoint Research and Management Science." *Journal of Management Inquiry*, 1994, 3(1), 74–82.

Fletcher, Joyce K. "Personal Development in the New Organization: A Relational Approach to Developing the Protean Worker." In Douglas T. Hall (ed.), *The Career Is Dead—Long Live the Career*. San Francisco: Jossey Bass, 1996.

Fletcher, Joyce K. *Relational Theory in the Workplace*. Wellesley, Mass.: Stone Center, Wellesley Centers for Women, Wellesley College, 1996.

Fletcher, Joyce K. "Relational Practice: A Feminist Reconstruction of Work." *Journal of Management Inquiry*, 1998, 7, 163–186.

Fletcher, Joyce K., *Disappearing Acts: Gender, Power and Relational Practice at Work*. Cambridge, Mass.: MIT Press, 1999.

Fletcher, Joyce K., and Roy Jacques. *Relational Practice: An Emerging Stream of Theory and Its Significance*. Boston: Center for Gender in Organizations, Simmons Graduate School of Management, 1999.

Fletcher, Joyce K., Jean B. Miller, and Judith V. Jordan. "Women and the Workplace: Applications of the Psychodynamic Theory." *American Journal of Psychoanalysis*, 2000, 60, 243–262.

Ford Foundation. *Men and Women at Home and in the Workplace: Current Debates and Future Directions*. New York: Ford Foundation, 1989.

Ford Foundation. *Work and Family Responsibilities: Achieving A Balance*. New York: Ford Foundation, 1989.

Galinsky, Ellen, Stacy S. Kim, and James T. Bond. *Feeling Overworked: When Work Becomes Too Much*. Scarsdale, N.Y.: Families and Work Institute, 2001.

Greenwood, Davydd J., and Morten Levin. *Introduction to Action Research: Social Research for Social Change.* Thousand Oaks, Calif.: Sage, 1998.

Grover, Mary Beth. "Daddy Stress." *Forbes,* Sept. 6, 1999, pp. 202–208.

Hammonds, Keith H. "Family Values." *Fast Company,* Dec. 2000, pp. 169–182.

Hammonds, Keith H. "Practical Radicals." *Fast Company,* Sept. 2000, pp. 162–174.

Harrington, Mona. *Care and Equality: Inventing a New Family Politics.* New York: Knopf, 1999.

Hays, Sharon. *The Cultural Contradictions of Motherhood.* New Haven, Conn.: Yale University Press, 1996.

Hochschild, Arlie. *The Second Shift: Working Parents and the Revolution at Home.* New York: Viking, 1989.

Hochschild, Arlie. *The Time Bind: When Work Becomes Home and Home Becomes Work.* New York: Metropolitan Books, 1997.

Jacobson, Gary, and John Hillkirk. *Xerox: American Samurai.* New York: Collier, 1986.

Jordan, Judith V., Alexandra Kaplan, Jean B. Miller, Irene P. Stiver, and Janet Surrey (eds.). *Women's Growth in Connection.* New York: Guilford Press, 1991.

Kanter, Rosabeth M. *Men and Women of the Corporation.* New York: Basic Books, 1977.

Kanter, Rosabeth M. *Work and Family in the United States: A Critical Review and Agenda for Research and Policy.* New York: Russell Sage Foundation, 1977.

Kearns, David T., and David A. Nadler. *Prophets in the Dark: How Xerox Reinvented Itself and Beat Back the Japanese.* New York: HarperBusiness, 1992.

Kelleher, David, and Kirsten Moore. *Marginal to Mainstream: Scaling Up Gender and Organizational Change Interventions.*

Boston: Center for Gender in Organizations, Simmons Graduate School of Management, 1997.

Kolb, Deborah M. "Women's Work: Peacemaking in Organizations." In Deborah M. Kolb and Jean M. Bartunek (eds.), *Hidden Conflict in Organizations: Uncovering Behind-the-Scenes Disputes.* Thousand Oaks, Calif.: Sage, 1992.

Kolb, Deborah M., and Jean M. Bartunek (eds.). *Hidden Conflict in Organizations: Uncovering Behind-the-Scenes Disputes.* Thousand Oaks, Calif.: Sage, 1992.

Kolb, Deborah M., and Judith Williams. *The Shadow Negotiation: How Women Can Master the Hidden Agendas That Determine Bargaining Success.* New York: Simon & Schuster, 2000.

Kolb, Deborah M., Joyce K. Fletcher, Debra E. Meyerson, Deborah Merrill-Sands, and Robin J. Ely. *Making Change: A Framework for Promoting Gender Equity in Organizations.* Boston: Center for Gender in Organizations, Simmons Graduate School of Management, 1998.

Krasner, Jeffrey. "Hitting the Glass Ceiling." *Boston Sunday Globe,* May 30, 2000, p. G1.

Laslett, Barbara, and Rhona Rapoport. "Collaborative Interviewing and Interactive Research." *Journal of Marriage and the Family,* Nov. 1975, pp. 968–977.

Levine, James, and Todd L. Pittinsky. *Working Fathers: New Strategies for Balancing Work and Family.* Reading, Mass.: Addison-Wesley, 1997.

Massachusetts Institute of Technology. *A Study on the Status of Women Faculty in Science at MIT.* Cambridge, Mass.: Massachusetts Institute of Technology, 1999.

Meyerson, Debra E. *Tempered Radicals: How People Use Difference to Inspire Change at Work.* Boston: Harvard Business School Press, 2001.

Meyerson, Debra E., and Maureen Scully. *Tempered Radicalism: Changing the Workplace from Within.* Boston: Center for

Gender in Organizations, Simmons Graduate School of Management, 1999.

Meyerson, Debra E., and Joyce K. Fletcher. "A Modest Manifesto for Shattering the Glass Ceiling." *Harvard Business Review*, 2000, 78(1), 127–136.

Miller, Jean B. *Toward a New Psychology of Women.* Boston: Beacon Press, 1976.

Miller, Jean B., and Irene P. Stiver. *The Healing Connection: How Women Form Relationships in Therapy and in Life.* Boston: Beacon Press, 1997.

Mintz, Steven, and Susan Kellogg. *Domestic Revolutions: A Social History of Family Life.* New York: Free Press, 1988.

Moore, Robert, and Douglas Gillette. *King, Warrior, Magician, Lover: Rediscovering the Archetypes of the Mature Masculine.* New York: HarperCollins, 1990.

National Sleep Foundation. "Sleep in America, 2001." http://www.sleepfoundation.org/publications/2001poll.html. Mar. 2001.

Nelson, Julie A. "The Study of Choice or the Study of Provisioning? Gender and the Definition of Economics." In Marianne A. Ferber and Julie A. Nelson (eds.), *Beyond Economic Man: Feminist Theory and Economics.* Chicago: University of Chicago Press, 1993.

Parasuraman, Saroj, and Jeffrey H. Greenhaus (eds.). *Integrating Work and Family: Challenges and Choices for a Changing World.* Westport, Conn.: Quorum, 1997.

Perlow, Leslie A., Rhona Rapoport, Deborah M. Kolb, and Lotte Bailyn. "Working with Resistance: Notes on Changing Organizations to Enhance Gender Equity." Paper presented at the annual meeting of the Academy of Management, Dallas, Tex., Aug. 1994.

Raelin, Joe. "Preface." *Management Learning*, 1999, 30, 115–125.

Rao, Aruna, Rieky Stuart, and David Kelleher (eds.). *Gender at Work: Organizational Change for Equality.* West Hartford, Conn.: Kumarian Press, 1999.

Rapoport, Rhona. "Restructuring Work and Family." *Proceedings of the Einar Thorsrud Memorial Symposium.* Olso: Work Research Institute, 1987.

Rapoport, Rhona. "Men's Involvement as Fathers in the Care of Children: Possibilities of Change in the Workplace." *European Childcare Network Services,* 1990.

Rapoport, Rhona, with Peter Moss. *Men and Women as Equals at Work.* London: Thomas Coram Research Unit, 1990.

Rapoport, Rhona, and Robert N. Rapoport. *Dual-Career Families.* Harmondsworth, England: Penguin, 1971.

Rapoport, Rhona, and Robert N. Rapoport. "Men, Women, and Equity." *Family Coordinator,* Oct. 1975, pp. 421–432.

Rapoport, Rhona, and Robert N. Rapoport. *Dual-Career Families Reexamined: New Integrations of Work and Family.* New York: HarperCollins, 1976.

Rapoport, Rhona, Lotte Bailyn, Deborah M. Kolb, and Joyce K. Fletcher, "Relinking Life and Work," *Systems Thinker,* 1998, 9(8), 1–5.

Rapoport, Robert N. "Three Dilemmas in Action Research." *Human Relations,* 1970, 23, 499–513.

Rapoport, Robert N., and Rhona Rapoport. "Work and Family in Contemporary Society." *American Sociological Review,* 1965, 30, 381.

Rapoport, Robert N., and Rhona Rapoport. "Dual-Career Families: The Evolution of a Concept." In Eric Trist and Hugh Murray (eds.), *The Social Engagement of Social Science: A Tavistock Anthology.* Philadelphia: University of Pennsylvania Press, 1989.

Rayman, Paula M. *Beyond the Bottom Line: The Search for Dignity at Work.* New York: Bedford/St. Martin's, 2001.

Reason, Peter, and Hilary Bradbury (eds.). *Handbook of Action Research: Participative Inquiry and Practice.* London: Sage, 2001.

Reich, Robert B. *The Future of Success.* New York: Knopf, 2001.

Rossi, Alice S. "Equality Between the Sexes: An Immodest Proposal." *Daedalus,* 1964, 93, 638–646.

Ruderman, Marian, and Patricia Ohlott. *Standing at the Cross-roads: Next Steps for Developing High-Achieving Women.* San Francisco: Jossey-Bass, 2002.

Russo, Francine. "Aggression Loses Some of Its Punch." *Time,* July 30, 2001, pp. 42–44.

Schein, Edgar H. *Organizational Culture and Leadership.* (2nd ed.) San Francisco: Jossey-Bass, 1992.

Schein, Edgar H. *Process Consultation Revisited: Building the Helping Relationship.* Reading, Mass.: Addison-Wesley, 1999.

Schor, Juliet. *The Overworked American: The Unexpected Decline of Leisure.* New York: Basic Books, 1991.

Senge, Peter. *The Fifth Discipline: The Art and Practice of the Learning Organization.* New York: Doubleday, 1990.

Senge, Peter, Art Kleiner, Charlotte Roberts, Richard Ross, George Roth, and Bryan Smith. *The Dance of Change: The Challenges to Sustaining Momentum in Learning Organizations.* New York: Doubleday, 1999.

Shalit, Ruth. "The Taming of the Shrews." *Elle,* Aug. 2001, pp. 102–109.

Sharkey, Joe. "Business Travel: The World Bank Gauges the Toll Travel Takes on Employees and Looks for Ways to Soften the Effect." *New York Times,* May 10, 2000, p. M1.

Sharpe, Rochelle. "As Leaders, Women Rule." *Business Week,* Nov. 20, 2000, pp. 75–84.

Sitkin, Sim B. "Learning Through Failure: The Strategy of Small Losses." *Research in Organizational Behavior,* 1992, *14,* 231–266.

Swamy, Anand, Young Lee, Stephen Knack, and Omar Azfar. *Gender and Corruption.* College Park: Center for Institutional Reform and the Informal Sector, University of Maryland, 1999.

Thomson, Elizabeth. "The Cost of Depression." *MIT Tech Talk,* Aug. 23, 2000, p. 3.

Tilghman, Shirley M. "Science vs. the Female Scientist." *New York Times*, Jan. 25, 1993.

Tilghman, Shirley M. "Science vs. Women: A Radical Solution." *New York Times*, Jan. 26, 1993.

United Nations Development Programme. "The Invisible Heart: Care and the Global Economy." In *Human Development Report, 1999*. New York: Oxford University Press, 1999.

Valian, Virginia. *Why So Slow? The Advancement of Women*. Cambridge, Mass.: MIT Press, 1997.

Weick, Karl. "Small Wins: Redefining the Scale of Social Problems." *American Psychologist*, 1984, 39(1), 40–49.

Whyte, William F., Davydd J. Greenwood, and Peter Lazes (eds.). *Participatory Action Research*. Thousand Oaks, Calif.: Sage, 1991.

Williams, Joan. *Unbending Gender: Why Family and Work Conflict and What to Do About It*. New York: Oxford University Press, 2000.

Index